CLASSROOM TO CEO IN 30 DAYS

AN EDUCATOR'S GUIDE TO START A PROFITABLE ONLINE SIDE HUSTLE

ERICA TERRY

EduMatch Publishing

To my mother, Veronica Crawford and my father, Johnny Crawford (may your soul rest in peace). Thank you for your unconditional love and support throughout my entire life.

To my hubby, Mel and our beautiful daughter, Eva. I am so lucky to be a part of Team Terry + 1. Your love pushes me to be my best self and motivates me to live out my dreams. I love you to the moon and back.

WAIT... THERE'S MORE!
WWW.CLASSROOMTOCEO.COM/30DAYS

Start a profitable online business in the next 30 days with the SIMPLE Classroom to CEO System! As a valued member of the Classroom to CEO Community, you get LIFETIME ACCESS to the companion course, which includes videos and tools to help you build your business, all at no additional cost to you.

Just visit this special web page for your free content upgrade so that you can set up your business, build a website, start your email list, attract paying customers, plus a whole lot more in the next 30 days.

www.classroomtoceo.com/30days

CONTENTS

INTRODUCTION

I failed.

Throughout my life, I have let the very thought of having to say those two words stop me from attempting to achieve my dreams.

High School: Dream to be in the high school's gospel choir...

I didn't want to say I failed, so I never tried out.

College: Dream to be a doctor...

I didn't want to have to look my father in the eyes and admit *I failed,* so after signing up for the MCAT several times, I never actually sat for the exam.

As you can see, I don't even have to actually fail something to have these words strike fear into my heart, and it's that fear in my heart that I've allowed to hold me back on so many occasions.

The recurring theme in my life has always been a fear of failure, and it didn't stop showing up after college.

Adult: Dream of publishing a book

Adult: Dream of being a keynote speaker at conferences

Adult: Dream of hosting a conference where thousands of educators lives are transformed

These are all dreams that I've had in my heart for YEARS and in my heart is where they've stayed…

Until Now.

In 2015, after a 10 year battle with infertility, I welcomed my daughter into the world. The moment they laid her on my chest, the tears began to flow, and the chains were broken. The fear of failure that had held me back for so long was lifted.

I knew that she deserved more.

She deserved more than a mommy who, as Chief Academic Officer of a statewide charter school, was stuck to her phone and laptop 16 hours per day.

She deserved more than a mommy who was away from home two or three days a week, traveling the state to visit the schools that she supervised.

She deserved more than the Teacher Retirement System would ever provide, no matter how high up the ladder I climbed.

She deserved a legacy.

By the time the doctor picked her up and passed her to the nurse to get weighed and cleaned, I knew that there was nothing more important than creating a life and legacy for her that her children and grandchildren would benefit from.

At that moment, I made the conscious decision to push past the fear so that I could walk into my divine destiny.

Now, while I can't say that fear doesn't still creep up from time to time (*you better believe that it does*), I have learned to recognize it for what it is and push past it. I no longer allow fear of failure to stop me from pursuing my dreams because achieving them is too important.

In the next 30 days, you are going to learn much more about how I was able to move past my fear of failure to begin achieving my adult dreams, but here's what I want you to know.

This book is not about me.

It's about you.

It's not about my life.

It's about your life.

It's not about my legacy.

It's about your legacy.

It's not about my dreams.

It's about your dreams.

You are not here right now reading this book so that you can learn about my life. Nope! You are here so that you can begin to transform yours.

This book will help you to do just that.

But you can only transform your life if you make the conscious decision right now to push past your fears so that you can walk into your purpose.

Maybe you're like me and find yourself not doing anything to move towards the goals that are hidden in your heart because you'd rather say that you don't want to do it than to give it a try and end up having to say those two dreaded words "I failed."

Have you allowed the Fear of Failure to hold you back from pursuing your dreams?

Ok… Fear of Failure may not be your thing, but is it a

Fear of Success…

Fear of the Unknown…

Fear of Abundance…

Fear of Lacking Knowledge…

What is your FEAR?

Over the next 30 days, I'm going to ask you to make one CEO Success Move a day. CEO Success Moves provide you with the opportunity to take action by applying the strategy that you learned in that day's lesson.

While I typically provide a CEO Success Move at the end of each chapter, right now, we are going to do a practice run because on the other side of fear is the life of your dreams.

On the other side of fear is your very profitable side hustle…

On the other side of fear is your best-selling book…

On the other side of fear is your online course…

On the other side of fear is your educational consulting and coaching program…

On the other side of fear is a life of freedom and flexibility that allows you to pee whenever the feeling hits without having to wait for a bell to ring…

But here's the deal, you can't get to the other side of fear unless you identify the fear that holds you back. When you know what that fear is, only then do you have the power to break the chains and knock it back down whenever it shows up in your life.

Because trust me, as you move along this path of edupreneurship, fear will arise in your heart, and I don't want that fear to stop you from creating a life that you love and the legacy your family deserves.

So let's do a practice run of a CEO Success Move right now. For this practice run, you are going to identify your greatest fear and after you finish this CEO Success Move, come back so that we can talk about how we're going to work together over the next 30 days to get you to the other side of that fear.

Sounds good?

Alright, let's do this!

Practice Making a CEO Success Move

Step 1 | Reflect upon each stage of your life — High School, College, Adult — and identify the dreams that you never pursued.

Step 2 | After you've identified your lost dreams, create a list of the fear(s) that stopped you from pursuing those dreams.

Got it?

Awesome. If you'd like to use an editable worksheet to complete the first two steps of this CEO Success Move, enroll now in the free companion course that's included with your book purchase by signing up at *www.classroomtoceo.com/30days*.

After you've taken time to identify the fear(s) that have stopped you from creating a life that you love, come on back so that I can share the final step of this practice CEO Success Move with you.

Welcome back!

Now that you've taken time to reflect on your life and have identified your fear(s), let's discuss what to do about it and complete the final step of today's CEO Success Move.

Life has taught me that the best cure to fear is action. It's making the decision that you're going to take daily action to create a life that you love waking up to that empowers you to conquer your fear.

That takes us to the final step of today's CEO Success Move.

Step 3 | Make a declaration that beginning today, you will not allow your fears to stop you from achieving your dreams

See my friend, the difference between where you are today, and where you deserve to be, is wrapped up in one word—ACTION.

It's taking action every single day that's going to allow you to be successful in starting your side hustle. Furthermore, it's continuing to show up daily and take action that's going to grow your side hustle to unbelievable heights.

Taking daily action despite being scared is what you've seen me practice every single day as I've built my side hustle, Classroom to CEO...

I started it while I was scared.

To tell you the truth, I'm still scared.

I'm scared to write this book, but I keep moving, I keep building, and I continue to push past the fear because I know that on the other side of fear is the life I've always dreamed of.

Make a promise to yourself and me that you will show up every single day for the next 30 days so that you can create the online side hustle that will allow all of your dreams to come true.

Promise that you will continue to move forward despite any challenges that arise.

Promise that you will keep building your business, even after our 30 days together comes to an end.

Promise that you will continue to push past the fear, EVERY. SINGLE. DAY.

Ok... Now that you've made your promises to show up and do the work, it's time for me to make a few of my own.

MY PROMISES TO YOU

First and foremost, I promise to always be honest and keep it real with you. I've always heard that you should write the book you want to read, and this is the book I wish I had when I first decided to start a side hustle. That was three years and several failed attempts ago (*which you'll hear much more about in the coming weeks*).

Yes, I failed, but each time I got back up, took everything I learned, and tried again. I kept trying until the day that I recognized that I wasn't just an educator with a side hustle. I was a CEO.

For me, being a CEO is about much more than owning a business. CEO in Classroom to CEO represents our manifesto:

We are Purpose Driven Edupreneurs that
Create multiple streams of income
Empower others to achieve success
Operate with a successful edupreneur mindset

Once I began operating as a CEO, I created four additional income streams in less than one year. With that being said, I promise to give you the good, bad, and ugly about my Classroom to CEO journey in this book.

Lastly, I promise that this book will be full of ideas, resources, and tips that you can apply immediately and in a short amount of time. As an educator, who is also an edupreneur, your time will be very limited, which is why I have designed this book to empower you to build a business in the next 30 days.

WHAT TO EXPECT:

This month you will discover how to use the SIMPLE 6 Step Classroom to CEO in 30 Days System to create an online business that allows you to use your unique gifts and talents to empower others to achieve success.

In the next 30 days, you will make the shift from an educator to an edupreneur mindset, start an online business as well as create your first product, even if you think that you lack the technical skills to make it happen. Trust me… it's not as hard as you think!

Over the next 30 days, you will implement the 6 steps that I cover in the SIMPLE Classroom to CEO in 30 Days System, which are:

1| Shift to a Successful Edupreneur Mindset (Days 1-5)
2| Identify One Problem to Solve (Day 6-10)
3| Make a CEO Success Plan (Days 11-13)
4| Produce a Solution-Focused Freebie + Product (Days 14-20)
5| List Build Like PROS (Days 21-25)
6| Engage as an Expert (Days 26-30)

CEO Success Moves:

Each day you will be asked to complete a CEO Success Move. If you're serious about building a successful side hustle, then I recommend that you set a daily one-hour appointment to read the chapter and complete your CEO Success Move. Some days you will finish in less than an hour. When that happens, move on to the next day's task and begin that work because other days may take longer than an hour.

Life happens. So don't fret if you don't finish the CEO Success Move for the day. It's ok. Come back to it the next day because, in the end, you'll be able to make all 30 CEO Success Moves within 30 days if you remain focused and dedicate at least one hour a day to show up and do the work.

Speaking of showing up and doing the work, at the end of each CEO Success Move, I ask you to not only show up but to also Show Out! Typically when you Show Out, you're asked to create a social media post that shares your progress, and I always ask that you tag me @ericaterryceo on Instagram and use the #ClassroomtoCEOin30days hashtag.

The reasons I ask you to tag me and use the #ClassroomtoCEOin30days hashtag are two-fold. First of all, I'm nosey. Don't blame me; it runs in the family. LOL! All jokes aside, I honestly am nosey, so I want you to tag me so that I can get all up in your business and see what you're up to each day.

Secondly and most importantly, I believe that one of the keys to achieving success as an edupreneur lies in having others hold you accountable and celebrate your successes with you. Not only do I want to be that person for you, but I also recommend that you invite one or two of your educator friends to join you along this 30-day journey.

My goal is to do more than simply write a book. I hope to inspire you to transform your life because you deserve to live the life that you've helped so many of your students to achieve.

When you Show Out, it lets me know that you're showing up, doing the work, and it allows me the opportunity to cheer you on, offer feedback, and if I notice that you're no longer showing out every day, trust and believe that I'll slide up in your DM's and call you out on it so that you can get back to work.

It is so important as a community of educators to hold each other accountable and celebrate every success. I promise to always hold you accountable and celebrate every success with you.

As you move further along in making CEO Success Moves, what you'll discover is that some of the tasks, like creating a digital resource or setting up an automated email system, are technical, but don't worry if you're not tech-savvy. I've got you covered!

FREE COMPANION COURSE

When you go to > *www.classroomtoceo.com/30days* < and sign up for the FREE Companion Course that is included with your book purchase, you'll discover video tutorials where I take you behind the scenes of Classroom to CEO and show you how to complete your CEO Success Moves.

You will also have access to editable social media images and other resources that empower you to start an online business and achieve success as an edupreneur.

Now that I've covered the basics, it's time for you to Show Out for the first time!

You Showed Up, Now It's Time for You to SHOW OUT!

Today you will Show Out by letting me know that you've committed to push past your fears and show up every day for the next 30 days. To do this, you will create a social media post where you share one of the promises that you made during your practice CEO Success Move.

Feel free to use the social media template included in the free companion course so that you don't have to spend a lot of time creating an image for the post on your own. Be sure to tag @ericaterryceo on Instagram and use the #ClassroomtoCEOin30days so that I can show your post some love.

I am so excited that you're here. I know that the online business that you will create this month is going to empower so many people to achieve success in their own lives. I can't wait to witness you walk into your purpose!

STEP 1 | SHIFT TO A SUCCESSFUL EDUPRENEUR MINDSET

DAY 1

DISCOVER THE PURPOSE OF YOUR
#EDUCATORPROBLEMS

For teachers all over the world, the 2019-2020 school year will forever go down as the most memorable year of their career. That was certainly the case for Paula Jackson.

Paula was a fourth-grade teacher at Revere Elementary School, and the group of fourth-graders on her team were what some would call a "difficult bunch." Behavior issues usually led to disruptions in every class period. While other teachers spent their time complaining about the students to anyone that would listen, Paula was too busy researching and implementing new classroom management strategies to do so. Paula spent the entire first semester refining her engagement strategies, and when Covid-19 came and shut her school down, she took this same approach to her virtual classroom.

Ask Paula, and she'll be the first to tell you that those first couple of weeks of teaching online were rough. Rather than complain, she stepped up to the challenge and spent time researching effective engagement strategies in the virtual classroom. After she found a few strategies that she believed would help her be more effective as a virtual classroom teacher, she began her process of implementing, tweaking, and implementing those strategies again and again until she got it right.

By the time her students returned from Spring Break in April, Paula was a rockstar teaching in a virtual learning environment. Her virtual classroom flowed just as smoothly as her physical one, but when she spoke with other teachers at her school and scrolled through her Facebook timeline, she realized that wasn't the case for a lot of her teacher friends. They were struggling to make virtual learning fun and engaging for their students, and she knew that she could help.

While she could have easily given away all of the resources that she'd created, Paula thoroughly enjoyed her experience of teaching from home, and out of nowhere came a desire to make her temporary at-home position a permanent one. She loved teaching and valued the relationships that she was able to make with her students and their families, but she also loved waking up fifteen minutes before her first class, putting on a decent shirt with her pajama pants, pushing the button on her Keurig to brew a cup of coffee, and turning on her laptop to get her day started. It was the life that she'd always dreamed of, and she was determined to make it a permanent situation.

Rather than giving away all of the resources that she'd created, she decided to turn her #EducatorProblem into an opportunity to make her dreams of becoming an edupreneur a reality. Paula started an online business and created a digital toolkit that empowered other teachers to actively engage students in a virtual environment. The best part is that her goals didn't take years to achieve. Using the SIMPLE Classroom to CEO in 30 Days System, she was able to plan, create resources, and launch her online business in one month.

Like Paula, I'm willing to bet that the 2019-2020 school year was a memorable one for you too. I'm sure that you encountered an #EducatorProblem or two yourself, and that was before Covid-19 arrived and completely turned your world upside down.

If you're shaking your head and saying to yourself, "Yes, girl! You're talking to me because I certainly had my share of #EducatorProblems," then let me start by assuring you that you're in the right place!

If your #EducatorProblems had you so stressed out that in 2020 when Covid-19 showed up at our doorstep and closed schools all across the world, you were secretly happy to be working from home, then you're in the right place!

If you found yourself at the end of summer 2020 adding a line to your prayers that schools wouldn't reopen in the fall, because even with the extended work from home spring semester, you still weren't ready for the school year to begin, then you're in the right place!

The next 30 days are going to completely transform your mindset so that you become less like those educators that spend their time complaining about their #EducatorProblems everywhere they go and become more like Paula. Paula operated with the successful edupreneur mindset that you'll discover over the next five days. She understood the value of focusing on solutions and then using those solutions to build a profitable online business.

As educators, the question is never do you have #EducatorProblems because you most certainly do.

I mean, seriously, in your years as an educator, how many times have you experienced feeling stressed out and overwhelmed about how your students would perform on their standardized test and how it would impact your effectiveness score? #EducatorProblems

How many times have you felt stressed out and overwhelmed by administrators that demanded you to do this and to do that? Then on top of this and that, they asked you to do something else without providing the tools and support that you needed to get this, that, and that too done. #EducatorProblems

How many times have you felt stressed out and overwhelmed by parents who were upset about their child's academic performance and would much rather blame you (or your staff) than take personal responsibility for helping their child do better? #EducatorProblems

How many times have you felt stressed out and overwhelmed from being required to attend a staff meeting before school, engage in professional learning during your planning period, and then attend an IEP meeting after school, all while still being expected to meet the demands of your job? #EducatorProblems

How stressed were you from the thought of having to return to school while the rates of Covid-19 infections were steadily rising? #EducatorProblems

How stressed are you from worrying about the impact of the economic downturn on school district budgets and what that will mean for your future paychecks? #EducatorProblems

#EducatorProblems. All of us have them, so the better question is, how do you respond to yours?

This question is an important one. How you respond to your #EducatorProblems is what's going to make the difference between you achieving success as an edupreneur or you forever feeling stressed out, overwhelmed, and miserable as an educator. It's the difference between your moving from the Classroom to CEO in the next 30 days or finding yourself stuck doing a job that no longer brings you joy.

When you recognize that within every #EducatorProblem, there's a secret purpose waiting to be discovered, your life will begin to change. Your focus will shift from the #EducatorProblem to finding a creative solution that works. You will continue tweaking that solution until you get it right, and when you do, that's when your dream will become a reality. That's when you will be able to start a side hustle where   you   help   other   educators   to   overcome   their

#EducatorProblems by sharing the exact solution that worked for you.

When you approach your #EducatorProblems with a purpose-driven mindset, no longer do you spend your days upset, frustrated, stressed out, and overwhelmed when you find yourself in an unfavorable situation. No longer are you in the copy room complaining about your situation. No longer are you carrying school problems home and losing sleep over them. No longer do you spend your time wondering why this is happening to you.

When you realize that your #EducatorProblems are an opportunity for you to serve and empower other educators to achieve success, you shift into an edupreneur mindset and become more like Paula. Rather than spending your time focused on how bad your situation is, you shift your focus and begin to concentrate on how you can make the situation better for others in your field. Your focus shifts from complaining about the #EducatorProblem to implementing strategies to solve it.

Instead of being stressed out and overwhelmed, you are thankful that you have an opportunity to discover a solution that has yet to be found. You spend your time researching and implementing strategies and protocols that are already available, and then you tweak, implement, repeat, tweak, implement, repeat until it works.

Once you find a creative solution that works, you're overjoyed—not because things have become easier for you, but because you're going to be able to help other educators that are struggling with that same #EducatorProblem and make their life better too!

Trust me when I tell you that you are not the only educator in the world experiencing the #EducatorProblem that you're going through right now. There are thousands of others out there that are experiencing it too, and they are waiting for you to share your unique solution so that their life and career can become better.

That's why when you begin to operate with a successful edupreneur mindset and understand that there is a purpose behind your #EducatorProblem; it creates an opportunity for you to achieve success by building a profitable online business.

That's why moving from the Classroom to CEO is so important. You're not starting a side hustle and building an online business just so that you can obtain financial freedom and flexibility. No! It's about so much more than that.

Moving from the Classroom to CEO is about using your unique gifts and talents to empower educators around the world to achieve success in their current role.

The title CEO in *Classroom to CEO* has absolutely nothing to do with you owning your own business. Being a CEO means that you're **C**ommitted to **E**mpowering **O**thers by providing solutions that improve the lives of other educators.

I need you to understand that the online business that you are going to start in the next 30 days is about much more than you being able to get out of the classroom and get rich. If your focus is solely on reaching your financial goals, then you'll never be able to build a business that brings in enough money for you to get out of the classroom.

Just like in the classroom, amazing teachers focus solely on helping their students achieve success. The same is true for edupreneurs. The most successful edupreneurs are focused solely on empowering other educators to achieve success.

To be successful as an edupreneur, your online business must be focused on serving other educators and empowering them to achieve greatness. When you can use your #EducatorProblems and the lessons you've learned from those experiences to help someone else, that's when you'll truly begin to walk in purpose and move from the Classroom to CEO.

"DEAR #EDUCATORPROBLEMS,

It's not me... it's you. And it's OVER."

CEO Success Move #1:

Discover the Purpose of Your
#EducatorProblems

During today's CEO Success Move, you will reflect on your career and identify the #EducatorProblems that have stressed you out the most. I walk you through exactly how to discover the purpose of your #EducatorProblems in the video that's included in Day 1 of the companion course.

YOU SHOWED UP.

NOW IT'S TIME TO SHOW OUT!

Congratulations on completing your CEO Success Move and discovering the purpose behind your #EducatorProblems! I am so very proud of you for showing up and doing the work!

Now that you're beginning to operate with an edupreneur mindset, it's time to share what you've discovered with the world. Inside of the companion course, you will find a social media image that you can share. In the post, communicate how you're feeling after making today's CEO Success Move, and be sure to tag me @ericaterryceo on Instagram + use the hashtag #ClassroomtoCEOin30days so that I can show your post some love.

DAY 2
START WITH ONE

Achieving success in your role as an educator requires that you multitask and juggle a lot of different balls at the same time. I'm pretty sure that you know exactly what I'm talking about.

As a high school biology teacher, I would have anywhere from 25-32 students in each class. Although they all had different learning styles, I was still expected to meet their individualized needs and design lessons that ensured that each one of them was able to master all of the standards. Not only was I required to have a complete understanding of the content that I taught each day, but I had to be able to break it down in different ways so that every student mastered the standard I was teaching. That meant that I had to be knowledgeable of the entire ninth-grade biology curriculum.

ALL. OF. IT.

I had to know everything and do everything to be successful as a teacher.

This principle doesn't apply only to me. I'm 100% sure that this was your experience too! I can be 100% sure because I know that when you decided to become an educator, you made that decision knowing that you'd never earn the salary of a doctor, lawyer, or politician. You did it because your greatest care and concern in the world was to ensure that all students had access to a quality education so that they could live better lives.

Am I right about you? Are you also willing to do whatever it takes to ensure your students' success, including constantly working nights and weekends to make it happen?

If so, raise your hand and give me a "Yes, girl! That's me!"

I see you!

While it's good that you have that type of dedication and drive, what I'm going to say next may be a hard pill to swallow, but I have to be honest with you...

Are you that amazing educator that cares so much about your students achieving success that you do whatever it takes to get the job done, including working nights and weekends?

Are you that amazing educator that's so dedicated to empowering others in your building to achieve greatness that you willingly help everyone else for free?

Are you that amazing educator that's great at multitasking and getting stuff done so everyone comes and asks you to be on their team, and you find yourself always saying yes?

If you answered yes to any of these questions, then you have an amazing educator mindset, and that's great, but here's what you need to know...

If you continue to operate with the same mindset that has made you the amazing educator that you are, you will have a very difficult road to achieving success as an edupreneur.

Yep, you read that right. THAT amazing educator mindset that you have leads to failure as an edupreneur.

That's why today, I'm sharing one mindset shift that will have a huge impact on your Classroom to CEO journey.

Educators, out of the kindness of their good hearts, work before school, after school, and on weekends and expect nothing in return. The ability to multitask and do everything by yourself is what makes you great in your current role, but that same skill set and beliefs will kill your ability to achieve success as an edupreneur.

When I first began my edupreneur journey, I approached it with the exact same mindset that made me an amazing educator. I walked into the situation feeling like I had to know everything about online businesses and do everything on my own. I spent months researching how to start a website and how to earn money from an online business.

The research said I needed to have a website. At the time I was living on a teacher salary which meant that I couldn't afford to have a web designer create a website for me so what did I do? I taught myself how to create a website and I did it myself.

At that point, not only was I spending a lot of time researching how to start an online business, but I was spending even more time researching how to create a website. My research said the cheapest way to create a website was to use WordPress so I spent months learning WordPress in order to create my first website.

Once my website was finished, the research told me that I had to write a blog post every week. So what did I do? I began writing a blog post every week.

The research said that I should grow my email list. So what did I do? I spent time researching how to grow an email list. Then I spent time creating freebies so that I could attract an audience and add new subscribers to my email list.

The research said I had to share my weekly blog posts on social media. So what did I do? I created accounts for my business on several different social media platforms including, Facebook, Pinterest, Twitter, and Instagram. Then you know what I did next? I began posting every single day to every single platform.

The research said... I did...

At the end of all that researching and doing, can you guess what the final outcome was?

Yep, you guessed it!

I wasn't earning any money from my side hustle because not one of the many tasks that I spent my time diligently doing every day contributed to making my online business profitable.

Having a website with no products to sell = $0

Writing a weekly blog post with no products to sell = $0

Offering freebies to gain subscribers with no products to sell = $0

Posting to multiple social media platforms every day with no products to sell = $0

While being the CEO of an online business is not about the money, if you're not earning any money then you're not actually an edupreneur, are you? Nope! You're more of what I like to call an eduhobbyist.

If a hobby is what you're looking for, then start your business off by doing all of the things that I was doing when I first started, and a hobby is exactly what you'll have at the end of our 30-day journey.

But if becoming a successful edupreneur and moving from the Classroom to CEO is your ultimate goal, then heed my warning:

STOP TRYING TO KNOW AND DO EVERYTHING ON YOUR OWN!

I need for you to understand that to be successful as an edupreneur, you cannot approach it with the same mindset that makes you an amazing educator. You cannot try to teach yourself how to do everything and then go off and do it all on your own. I promise you that if you take that approach, it will eventually become way too much for you to handle. Trust me when I tell you that approach will leave you overwhelmed and frustrated.

Like educators, edupreneurs are willing to work on their business before school, after school, and on weekends, but to achieve success, they also set up systems that ensure that they get paid for their time and effort.

Don't make the mistake of thinking that just because you need products to earn money as an edupreneur, that if you create 100+ products and add them to your online store, then you'll automatically earn a lot of money. You don't know how many teacher sellers I know that have created and added tons of resources to their online store and still are not earning $100/month from their business. That add 100+ digital resources to your teacher resource marketplace store strategy doesn't work either!

To be successful as an edupreneur, you must always do these two things: keep it SIMPLE and start with ONE.

Start with solving ONE problem.
Start with ONE product.
Start with ONE type of content.
Start with ONE social media platform.

ALWAYS START WITH ONE!

By starting with ONE, you can focus on empowering other educators to achieve success while also building an online business that allows you to earn the additional money you need to live the life you and your family (or future family) deserve.

Don't spend your time worrying about trying to learn and do everything on your own right now. This book will teach you everything you need to know to start a side hustle and structure it in a way that makes it profitable.

As your online business grows and the money starts to roll in, that's when you can add virtual assistants to your team that will help you expand and reach new heights. For example, if you start building your social media platform on Facebook and gain an audience there, when you begin earning money from the ONE product that you'll create during this 30-day journey, then you will use some of that money to hire a virtual assistant to build your Instagram account.

Just like in education, trying to do it all by yourself leads to overwhelm, which leads to burnout. I don't want that for you, so let's work together to build your side hustle with a solid foundation so that no matter what storm (or virus) comes your way, your online business always stands.

CEO Success Move #2:
Start with ONE

I know that you're ready to jump in and choose your business name, create products, and launch it to the world. Trust me, within this 30-day journey, we are going to accomplish all of those goals.

Before we do though, I want you to take some time today to identify your ONE. Then when the time comes for you to begin implementing that specific area of your business, you'll know exactly what you're going to do.

Identify your ONE social media platform, content, and product. Identify your ONE in each area, and then come back here so that you can Show Out!

YOU SHOWED UP.
NOW IT'S TIME TO SHOW OUT!

Congratulations on your decision to Start with ONE! I am so very proud of you for showing up and doing the work!

Now that you've decided what you're going to do, it's time to put it in the atmosphere and make a declaration to the world. Create a social media post that shares ONE of the choices that you made today. It can be as simple as a post that says, "I'm starting a podcast this year."

Don't worry about sharing the details because you haven't figured anything out yet. Simply state what you're planning to do and tag me @ericaterryceo on Instagram + use the hashtag #ClassroomtoCEOin30days so that I can show your post some love.

DAY 3
EDUPRENEUR SUCCESS ROUTINE

*O*MG! *My to-do list has 100 items on it, and I'm never able to get everything done!*

During the early days of my edupreneurial journey, that was the recurring theme of my life.

"Never Done" was my anthem. As was "Always Busy" and "No Time for Anything Else."

I was working my 9-5 (really 8-4) as a consultant for the Department of Education, and then I would come home and work on my business. Not only was the clickety-clack sound of my fingers hitting the keys to my laptop my constant companion, but my mind was always working because even in my sleep, I was thinking about what I needed to do next.

Reality didn't hit me until Christmas when my 3-year-old daughter was asked what she wanted, and she quickly replied, "a laptop so that I can be like my Mommy."

Wow! There I was, spending night and day working hard to build an online business so that I could create a legacy for her, and the only thing she saw was that I was constantly in front of my laptop.

Thoughts of me always sitting in front of my computer weren't what I wanted my daughter to have as childhood memories, so I knew that something had to change. There was no point in building a legacy for my daughter if I wasn't going to spend just as much time building a relationship with her. The last thing I wanted was to leave a legacy that provided her with material stuff from a mom that she never got to know or spend time with. I had to get my priorities straight, and I had to do it fast!

So I took it back to the basics and created a priority list. Prioritizing my life meant putting things in the right order.

God. Family. Business.

In that order.

With my priority list in hand, I established a daily routine that ensured that I would always keep first things first. Here's how my daily routine plays out from day to day.

God first means that an alarm is set for me to wake up early enough to spend time reflecting upon scriptures that keep me focused on the goals that I've set for the year. They help me to envision my future and motivate me to keep moving forward even when it feels like the odds are stacked against me. Lastly, I spend time praying and seeking God's infinite wisdom. This is the morning routine that I engage in daily before I do anything else. Ever since I've started this practice, I have experienced much more clarity and focus when it comes to the work that I do in my online business.

Family second means that when my daughter wakes up, I stop working to spend time with her. That means hugging and loving on her every morning. That means making sure that she has more than a

Pop-Tart for breakfast. It means on the weekends when she says, "Mommy, can you come to play with me?" I say "yes" even if it means that I have to stop in the middle of creating a new product or drafting my weekly newsletter.

Business third means that I wake up early enough in the morning that after I spend time with God, I have time to work on my business before my daughter wakes up. It means that I make time to work on my business every day, and I commit to working for at least one hour a day.

Yep, you read that right. I work on building my online business EVERY. SINGLE. DAY.

Why do I feel like it's necessary for me to show up and do the work every single day? I'm glad you asked!

Showing up and engaging in meaningful work each and every day is exactly what it takes to get to the next level that both you and I are trying to go to. That's what it takes to empower and positively impact the lives of educators all around the world. That's what it takes to build an online business that consistently generates income from multiple revenue streams every month. That's what it takes to create a legacy for our children. Showing up and doing the work every day for at least one hour a day is exactly what it takes to achieve success as an edupreneur.

Once I prioritized my life and used that priority list to establish my daily routine, everything changed.

No longer was I stressed out and overwhelmed because I had so many different tasks to complete all at the same time. I focused on doing the best I could with the time that I had and trusted that everything else would come in due season.

God. Family. Business. That's my priority list.

Though that may not be the order of your priority list or even the items on your priority list, an important factor to achieving success as an edupreneur is that you clearly establish your priorities so that you don't get so caught up in building your online business that you lose sight of what or who is most important in your life.

> # CEO Success Move #3:
> ## Get Your Priorities Straight!

Achieving success as an edupreneur requires you to have your priorities in the right order.

Once you have your priorities outlined, the next step is to structure your day in a way that ensures that you always keep first things first.

With that being said, today's CEO Success Move is twofold:

Step 1 | Create a priority list

Step 2 | Use the list that you created in Step 1 to establish a daily routine that keeps you focused on those things that are most important.

If you have some additional time, I highly recommend that you begin creating a list of your favorite quotes and/or scriptures that inspire you to continue pursuing your dreams even when it seems impossible.

YOU SHOWED UP.

NOW IT'S TIME TO SHOW OUT!

Congratulations on getting your priorities straight and making the decision to put first things first! I am so very proud of you for showing up and doing the work!

Now that you understand how you will keep what's most important at the forefront of your daily routine, it's time to share it with the world. Create a social media post that highlights one of your priorities. This may be a picture of your family or a quote image. Whichever way you decide to express this is completely up to you, but don't forget to tag me @ericaterryceo on Instagram + use the hashtag #ClassroomtoCEOin30days so that I can show your post some love.

DAY 4

EDUPRENEUR VISION OF SUCCESS

When January 1, 2020, arrived, I was entering my third year, having made several attempts to be a successful edupreneur, and I still hadn't completely figured it out yet. Even though I had created multiple streams of income so that my online side hustle was bringing in extra income every month, it was just enough to make me feel like I was approaching the door to success, but not enough to quite yet make me feel successful as an edupreneur.

I was close to success, but I hadn't quite reached the level of success that I knew was possible for edupreneurs, so I made the declaration that 2020 would be the year that I took my side hustle to the next level, and I sent the following email to everyone on my list.

Subj: It was a New year & I was depressed with eyes full of tears

4 years ago, on January 1, 2016, I recall vividly ringing in the new year devastated and depressed with eyes full of tears.

I was a brand new Mommy, and my maternity leave was OVER.

The new year meant that it was time for me to return to work & despite the fact that I had "made it" to Chief Academic Officer, I still had NO DESIRE to leave my 6-week old baby in the hands of a daycare provider that I didn't know so that I could return to a job that I couldn't stand.

My #TeacherProblems had turned into #AdminProblems & the very thought of having to go back to hell (at least that's what it felt like) made me sick to my stomach. Then to have to leave my baby on top of that was an absolute living nightmare!

At that moment, I was faced with a decision —keep feeling depressed, but be content because I was moving up the administrative ladder & earning six figures or toss my depression & that six-figure job aside to create the life of my dreams.

I chose the latter and made a commitment to focus on creating a legacy so that I could have the freedom & flexibility to always put my family first & be present for everything that my daughter does.

I'll be honest. It was the hardest decision of my life. I'd worked so hard (and accrued so much student loan debt) to get out of the classroom. I'd worked my way up the administrative ladder all the way to Chief Academic Officer, and I wondered how could I give it all up.

I was SO scared. I was choosing myself, choosing my family, choosing to make my dream life a reality — and I was scared out of my mind.

See, I was worried that I would fail. Fear of failure is a real thing, and I almost let it stop me from pursuing my dreams, but I looked into my daughter's eyes and instantly knew that she deserved more.

She deserved to have a mommy that wasn't stuck at the school late because an IEP meeting ran over or a parent came in at the end of the day and demanded to talk to someone NOW.

She deserved to have a mommy that didn't work all day, then was tied to her laptop all night to finish the extra work at home that she couldn't get done during normal work hours.

She deserved to have a mommy that wasn't so tired and stressed out at the end of the day that there wasn't much energy left for anyone else by the time she got home.

So when I was struck with the fear of failure and too afraid to choose myself, I chose my daughter, and it was the best choice that I have ever made.

Fast forward four years, and today, January 1, 2020, I rang in the new year with tears of joy because I'd surpassed my goal of creating 3 additional streams of income in 2019 and actually created 4. Through my biz, I was able to earn money from printable resources, courses, coaching, and affiliate marketing in 2019. Praise God!

I'm not going to lie to you; being an edupreneur is HARD WORK. I feel like I'm on my laptop morning, noon and night, but when my daughter says, "Mommy, can you play with me," I'm able to stop working and answer, "yes."

When she has an event going on at school, I'm able to adjust my calendar so that I can be there.

When she wakes up feeling sick, I'm able to stay home with her and take her to the doctor without having to worry about what'll happen or what won't happen at the school because I'm not there.

So while being an edupreneur is time-consuming and a lot of work, it's worth it.

On this first day of this new decade, I want you to walk into it confidently knowing that YOU. ARE. WORTHY. OF. SUCCESS.

YOUR FAMILY deserves to have the best of you.

And YOU deserve to live the life that you've always dreamed of.

Let's do this!

~Erica

I wrote the above email just as much for myself as I did for the people that were on my email list. January 1, 2020, there I was ringing in a new decade while standing at the front door of my edupreneur dream, and yet I was afraid to knock so that the door could be opened for me.

You see, I'd spent the majority of 2019 trying to figure out how to earn additional money by creating multiple streams of income, but what I discovered is that was only half the battle. I was getting that paper, but there was still something missing. I had failed to break through that invisible barrier that was holding me back and keeping me from achieving the level of success that I knew was possible.

After weeks of toying with the question of 'What's missing from my side hustle' and playing this equation '_____ + Paper = Side Hustle Success,' it finally hit me like a ton of bricks.

People, that's what's missing from my equation!

People + Paper = Side Hustle Success

Let me pause right here and give a quick Ebonics lesson. If you're looking around confused and trying to figure out how in the world is a piece of paper going to help you achieve success as an edupreneur, let me explain.

In Ebonics, paper = money (i.e., multiple streams of income)

2019 had taught me that getting paper was the easy part. I was able to earn money from multiple streams of income by implementing affiliate marketing strategies and offering courses and coaching services, but there was still something missing.

The discovery that I made that I am sharing with you today is that the ultimate key to achieving success as an edupreneur is to focus your time and energy on empowering others rather than focusing on how to earn more money from your side hustle.

When you keep your eye on the money, there never seems to be enough, but when you shift your gaze and truly focus on empowering others, the money flows in like a steady stream of water.

Even more, if you're not making a positive impact in the lives of people, then there's no purpose to you being the CEO of an online business.

But here's the deal…

Your mind will try to convince you that you don't have enough knowledge, expertise, or followers to make a positive impact in the lives of other educators, and that's simply not true.

As you begin to build the online business that you're creating this month, what's going to happen is that the more you empower educators to overcome their #EducatorProblems, the more you're going to be looked at as an expert in your field.

You're going to look up, and all of a sudden, doors will begin to open that are greater than anything you ever could have imagined.

Right now, you may be saying to yourself, "*There's no way that can happen to me.*"

My question to you is this, "Why not you?"

With less than 100 Facebook followers and a little over 1000 Instagram followers, I was able to secure multiple book deals, guest spots on my favorite podcasts, and multiple invitations to speak at conferences. If it can happen for me, I know without a doubt that the same can and will happen for you.

When it does, you must have a clear vision of success; otherwise, you will find yourself saying 'yes' to every opportunity that comes your way. You'll find yourself running through every door that has a money sign, every door that will give you the appearance of influence, every door that can make you look back and show all of the nay-sayers that they were wrong about you.

When you begin to run through every open door, you will quickly discover that you are further away from the people, and things that you said during yesterday's CEO Success Move matter most to you.

Today's lesson is designed to help you further clarify your priorities so that you can truly focus on the outcomes that you want to achieve from your side hustle. Having this type of clarity about what success looks like to you will empower you to take the online business that you're creating this month to the next level.

Becoming an edupreneur and building an online business will allow you the opportunity to earn more money than you can in your current role, but why is that important to you? What will earning more money as an edupreneur allow you to do (or have) that's different than what you've already got? Those are just some of the questions that you will answer as you make today's CEO Success Move.

Today you are going to create your Edupreneur Vision of Success. The Vision of Success that you are going to create today is not some fancy vision board that's going to take hours to complete.

Nope, it's simply a list of statements that all begin with "I know I'm a successful edupreneur when..."

When I first completed this CEO Success Move, it helped me to further refine the priority list and daily success routine that I shared with you yesterday. Recall from yesterday's lesson that I start every day off by reading scriptures and reflecting on my goals. Well, the final act of every day before I begin to dive into working on my business is to review the ten items that are on my Edupreneur Vision of Success list. It not only helped me to define what success means and looks like for me, but it gives me the power to say 'no' to any opportunities that present themselves which don't align with my vision of success.

Your Edupreneur Vision of Success is about you, not your online business. You must ask yourself the question, "What do I want success to look like in my life?"

As you know, my priorities are God. Family. Business. My Edupreneur Vision of Success includes a list of 10 statements that reflect those priorities.

Well, at least most of them do.

I'll be honest and admit that I tossed in a few that fulfill personal desires that may not necessarily be aligned with those three main values. But hey, my side hustle allows me to create a life that I love, so it's important for me to define exactly what that life looks like to me. Wouldn't you agree? *Work Hard, Play Hard* by Wiz Khalifa is my inner theme song. Lol!

Alright, let's do this!

To get your creative juices flowing, I've included statements from my Edupreneur Vision of Success below. You'll find my complete list in Day 4 of the companion course, but here are a few to get you started:

I'll know I'm a successful edupreneur when…

1. I have time every morning to spend developing a closer relationship with God through reading scriptures, reflection and prayer because I'm not in a rush to beat the bell or clock in on time
2. My online business enables me to create opportunities for others and be a blessing to my family members and close friends so that they too no longer have to worry about money
3. I spend 100% my time inspiring others to take action to build a legacy and create a life that they love waking up to on Monday mornings because all of the technical stuff is delegated to my team\

For me, success means that I have a close relationship with God, time to care for my family and that I'm able to bless others with my knowledge and wealth.

So my question for you is… What will success look like in your life?

That's the question that you're going to answer as you create your Edupreneur Vision of Success during today's CEO Success Move.

CEO Success Move #4:

Create Your Edupreneur Vision of Success

Today you will create a vision of success for your life as an edupreneur.

There is no specific number of items that you must include in your Edupreneur Vision of Success. Make it as long or as short as you'd like.

My only recommendation is that you include at least one item that you've already achieved. Doing so will allow you to feel a sense of accomplishment daily. It also contributes to the inner confidence of knowing that because you're already successful in at least one area, success in those other areas will come in due season. For me, my ability to wake up early enough every morning to spend time with God was a success criterion that I was able to easily achieve.

Enough about me. It's your turn! What does success as an edupreneur look and feel like for you?

YOU SHOWED UP.

NOW IT'S TIME TO SHOW OUT!

Today you will Show Out by creating a post that shares at least one of the elements in your Edupreneur Vision of Success. As always, tag me @ericaterryceo on Instagram + use the hashtag #ClassroomtoCEOin30days so that I can show your post some love.

DAY 5
3 LIES THAT CAN STOP YOU FROM ACHIEVING EDUPRENEUR SUCCESS

L et me start today off by first commending you on the work that you've done this week to develop a Successful Edupreneur Mindset.

When you first sat down to read this book, did you ever imagine that in less than one week, you would craft a complete vision for your life?

I think not!

But here you are. You did it! Congratulations!!!!!

Tomorrow is a big day for you! It's the first day that we will work together to start your side hustle and grow your online business. I'm so excited to begin this journey with you because I know that your online business will transform lives all around the world. As you spend more of your time empowering others, your life will begin to change for the better.

You will experience the freedom to pee whenever the feeling hits without having to wait for a bell to ring.

You will experience the freedom to stay home with your sick child without having to worry about whether or not the sub is implementing your lesson plans correctly or what's happening/not happening in your school because you're not there.

You will experience the pure joy of absolutely LOVING what you do so much that when you get ready for bed on Sunday night, rather than having the Sunday Night Blues, you're excited about the potential that Monday brings with it. As an edupreneur, a new day means a new opportunity to use your unique gifts and talents to empower others.

You will experience waking up in the morning and checking your email only to discover that you made a sale and earned money while you were sleeping. #SleepCoin

But here's the deal: You will never experience the freedom, flexibility, and unlimited earning potential that edupreneurship brings unless you continue to move forward on this journey by showing up and making CEO Success Moves EVERY. SINGLE. DAY.

I cannot tell you how many educators I've met that have million-dollar ideas but have not taken one single action step to bring any of those ideas to life. They make all kinds of excuses, but the two that I hear most often are…

I don't have enough time to start a side hustle and…

I don't have enough money to start an online business.

When it comes to not having enough time to start your side hustle, the only advice that I have is to MAKE THE TIME!

This book empowers you to become an edupreneur by spending at least ONE HOUR A DAY working on your business. So if that means waking up early, going to bed late, cutting off the TV, or hanging up the phone, DO IT!

With big dreams and a big purpose comes a big sacrifice. You're going to have to make a big sacrifice to create the time that you need to start a profitable online side hustle. Decide what that sacrifice will be and commit to creating a life that you love waking up to on Monday mornings.

That takes me to the second excuse that I hear from people with big dreams that haven't started their business yet, and that's, "I don't have enough money."

Before I get on my soapbox, let me preface what I'm about to say by first letting you know that I understand what it means to be a broke teacher.

I entered the field of education as a high school Biology teacher with a master's degree and a starting salary of $35,500. My student loans were more than my salary! I spent the first five years of my career working multiple part-time jobs, teaching summer school, and sponsoring after school clubs just to make ends meet.

So when you say that the struggle is real, trust me, I get it.

You may be a parent trying to figure out how to give your children a better life, and your salary is just not cutting it.

You may be a mom with young children who'd much rather be able to work from home so that you can spend more time nurturing and providing for your family's needs rather than being so exhausted at the end of the school day that you barely have enough energy to help with homework... but your family needs your salary to survive.

You may be a dad that wants the freedom to show up at every practice and football game, but without the extra money that you earn from coaching at your school, you won't be able to afford the sports team fees and all of the extra money associated with extracurricular activities for your children.

When you look at your bank account balance, you may truly believe that you don't have enough money to start an online business, but I stopped by to tell you that's simply not true.

Those doubts and fears that you feel is your Broke Educator Mindset trying to get in the way of your future as a successful edupreneur.

It's your Broke Educator Mindset that makes you believe that you don't have enough money to start a side hustle because you can't afford to create and maintain a website.

It's your Broke Educator Mindset that makes you believe that you don't have enough money to start a side hustle because you can't afford the software and tools that you'll need to create products.

It's your Broke Educator Mindset that makes you believe that you don't have enough money to start a side hustle because you can't afford to run ads to attract and grow an engaged online community.

If you let it, your Broke Educator Mindset will convince you that you don't have enough money to do this or that, and then you end up not doing anything at all.

Everything that your Broke Educator Mindset is trying to convince you of is lies, all lies!

"I don't have enough money to create and maintain a website."

That's Lie #1!

The Classroom to CEO in 30 Days System empowers you to start an online business with a free website tool, so you don't need money for that.

"I don't have enough money to purchase the software and tools that I need to create products."

That's Lie #2!

The Classroom to CEO in 30 Days System empowers you to create products with free tools readily available on the internet.

"I don't have enough money to run ads to attract and grow an engaged online community."

That's Lie #3!

The Classroom to CEO in 30 Days System empowers you to engage as an expert and grow your online community without spending a dime on ads.

Let me tell you something… not only do you have enough money to start a successful and profitable online side hustle, but you also have enough knowledge, expertise, and experience to build a business that truly impacts the lives of others.

There's a gift inside of you that you've successfully used to inspire your students to work hard to achieve their goals, and it's that same gift that's going to help you to transform the lives of other educators all over the world.

There's an educator that's struggling and needs YOUR unique gifts and talents! She needs to hear how you've struggled as an educator but were able to overcome it. She needs to know that you did it so that she can walk with the confidence of knowing that she can do it too!

If you've been putting off starting an online business and saying stuff like, "I ain't got the money" or "I ain't got no time to be doing all of that," then get ready to take the first step. Today's CEO Success Move will move you one step closer to pursuing your edupreneurial dreams so that you can make a great impact in the lives of others.

During today's CEO Success Move, you will implement specific steps to overcome the Broke Educator Mindset that has stopped you from pursuing your dreams.

While you may believe that this has nothing to do with your overall success as an edupreneur, there's nothing further from the truth.

The Broke Educator Mindset tends to creep in and show up right at the moment that you're beginning to gain momentum and experience growth in your business. It's at the point that you're standing at the doorway to your next level as an edupreneur that the Broke Educator Mindset makes its appearance and tries to stop you from taking that next step.

I share the story of how the Broke Educator Mindset hindered my online business growth in Episode 7 of the Classroom to CEO Podcast. We're also addressing it with today's CEO Success Move so that you're able to overcome it before it creeps up on you.

Are you ready to bust out of your Broke Educator Mindset?

Awesome! Let's do this!

CEO Success Move #5:

Bust out of your Broke Educator Mindset

Today's CEO Success Move is designed to empower you to break free from your Broke Educator Mindset. Inside of Day 5 of the companion course, you will discover a video where I break down the three-step strategy that I use to conquer a Broke Educator Mindset.

After you complete each step, come on back here so that you can Show Out!

YOU SHOWED UP.

NOW IT'S TIME TO SHOW OUT!

Depending on the nature of your experiences, busting out of a Broke Educator Mindset can be very personal and private. I would never ask you to divulge such a personal experience to the world in a social media post, so today let's make it a little fun.

Choose a song or a quote that you can reference to help you overcome a Broke Educator Mindset when it begins to creep up on you.

Need Ideas? In the companion course, I've included my playlist so that you can take a song from there or feel free to add a song to the list. I'm always looking for great music to uplift me when I feel down.

Once you've chosen your song or quote, create a post that shares it. Don't forget to tag me @ericaterryceo on Instagram and use the hashtag #ClassroomtoCEOin30days so that I can show your post some love. Remember, you don't have to say anything about a Broke Educator Mindset or your experiences in this post. Feel free to keep it completely about the music because when I see it, I'll know exactly what it's about. I can't wait to add your song to my playlist!

STEP 2 | IDENTIFY ONE PROBLEM TO SOLVE

DAY 6
MO' PROBLEMS ≠ MO' MONEY

After school meetings that could have been emails...
Disrespectful students and parents...
Excessive and redundant paperwork...
Co-workers who are bullies...
Sacrificing family time for late-night grading and lesson planning...

These are examples of real #EducatorProblems that were shared in response to a post that I made which simply said, "Name the #1 #TeacherProblem that you wish you could leave behind."

There were hundreds of responses to that simple post, which confirmed for me what I've been saying: ALL educators experience #EducatorProblems at one point or another during their career.

If you're an educator, then it isn't a matter of whether or not you have experienced #EducatorProblems.

The real question is "What are you going to do about it when #EducatorProblems arise?"

You can let your #EducatorProblems stress you out...

You can go on Facebook and complain...

You can spend EVERY. SINGLE. DAY. dreaming of quitting your job...

OR

You can flip the script and turn that negative into a positive...

You can use your #EducatorProblem as an opportunity to create the life of your dreams...

You CAN make the shift from #EducatorProblems to Edupreneur.

Believe it or not, your purpose lies in helping other educators to solve the same #EducatorProblems that you've struggled with yourself.

You're probably reading this and thinking that I'm crazy for even suggesting that you can use your #EducatorProblems to start a profitable online side hustle.

I get it because when I reflect upon my first-year teaching, I never would have imagined that years later I'd be leading PD as an educational consultant that empowers co-teachers to build strong relationships and transform instruction to meet the needs of all students.

I recall the weeks leading up to the first day of pre-planning as a first-year teacher, excitedly wondering what subject I'd be teaching. Would it be Biology which I loved, Physical Science which I understood but didn't like at all, or a combination of the two?

The moment I received my schedule, I realized that I'd been asking the wrong questions. It wasn't what I'd be teaching that I should have been wondering about. The better question would have been, 'Where will I be teaching?' To my surprise, I wasn't assigned to teach in a single classroom; I was assigned to three!

As if it wasn't bad enough that I would be floating to three different classrooms, the next surprise was that I wouldn't be teaching alone in those three classrooms, none of which were mine. I had a co-teacher, and we would be co-teaching in a classroom that didn't belong to either one of us! Talk about #EducatorProblems!

I had just finished a master's level educator prep program, and though it taught me a lot, it taught me absolutely nothing about how to successfully co-teach biology while floating between three different classrooms, pushing a cart filled with lab supplies through a crowded hallway in a high school of two thousand students.

Needless to say that between co-teaching and floating, I was completely stressed out and had a plethora of #EducatorProblems.

If someone had told me back then that I would go on to create an online business that empowers co-teachers to achieve success, I would have NEVER believed it! Co-teaching was the one area of teaching that hands-down brought me the most stress.

I was stressed out because I found myself co-teaching classes that were difficult to manage, and it felt like I was carrying the majority of the workload alone.

I was stressed out because there was no time to co-plan with my co-teacher.

I was stressed out because I was planning and then teaching all of the lessons by myself.

I was stressed out because I was grading most of the papers by myself.

To say I was stressed during my first year of teaching is an understatement. I was stressed out to the max!

When I think about the years that I spent as a classroom teacher, the truth of the matter is that there were a lot of #EducatorProblems that I could have used to build an online business. But because I understand the Power of ONE, I narrowed it down and chose to focus my side hustle on solving one main problem.

As you recall from Day 2, to be successful as an edupreneur, the two things that you must always remember is to keep it SIMPLE and always start with ONE.

Start with solving ONE Problem.

Start with ONE product.

Start with ONE type of content.

Start with ONE social media platform.

ALWAYS START WITH ONE!

Before we get to your CEO Success Move today, I want you to begin thinking about the area of education that has stressed you out the most.

If it was a problem for you, then trust me when I tell you that it's also a problem for thousands of other educators out there. Those educators that are struggling right now need your solution to make their life easier and in less than 30 days, they'll be able to have access to your solution because you will be sharing it when you launch your new online business.

Before we get started on building your online business, let me give you a warning.

I need you to really hear me on this, so listen up… Everyone in the back, can you hear me?...

Being in education for the past 18 years, I know without a doubt that you've experienced your share of #EducatorProblems. You may think that you can solve them all, and your mind will try to convince you that the more problems you help others to solve, the more money you'll make. But let me tell you right here, right now, that is NOT how this works.

Mo' Problems ≠ Mo' Money

Let me say that again...

Solving More Problems Does NOT Earn You More Money!

Take Ms. Jones, for example. Ms. Jones is a phenomenal third-grade teacher. In the seven years that she's been teaching, she's figured out very innovative strategies that have helped her students soar in reading, writing, and science. Since she's strong in all three areas, she thought that it was a great idea for her to start a store called *Ms. Jones 3rd Grade Resources Rock* and figured that she'd earn more money by creating reading, writing, and science resources. She spent her first nine months as an edupreneur working tirelessly to create enough reading, writing, and science resources to fill her store up. When she finally hit the magic number of 100 resources, she discovered that she still was not earning enough money to move out of the classroom, and she couldn't understand why.

Well, let me tell you why...

She was not earning anywhere near $1000 a month, even though she had 100 resources in her store because when someone landed on her site, they were confused. They weren't able to quickly figure out how the resources she created would benefit them. Just as quickly as they entered her store, they moved their mouse to the top right corner, hit the 'x,' and clicked off her store just as fast.

Since Ms. Jones was rocking and rolling as a third-grade teacher, she would have achieved much more success as an edupreneur by changing her approach. Her approach was to waste months creating writing AND reading AND science resources that hardly anyone bought.

A much better use of her time would have been to create a few awesome resources that made it easier for third-grade teachers to help students learn how to read. Not only would she have saved a lot of time, but she would have also empowered other teachers all over the world with the skills they needed to become a rockstar teacher in ONE area.

To ensure that this NEVER happens to you, today's CEO Success Move is going to require you to choose ONE Problem that you will begin building your online business around.

CEO Success Move #6:
Select ONE problem that your online
business will focus on solving.

Your CEO Success Move for today is to select ONE problem that your online business will solve.

In the days ahead, we will develop a clear, concise message and amazing resources that will attract educators, empower them to overcome this ONE problem, and turn them into paying customers.

> # YOU SHOWED UP.
> ## NOW IT'S TIME TO SHOW OUT!

Now that you've selected the first problem that you will solve through your side hustle, I want you to know that if this is an area that you're still struggling with at the moment, that's ok. This is the year that you will move past this #EducatorProblem because from this moment forward, you will shift your focus from the problem to the solution.

The best part is that you won't just be solving it for yourself. You'll be solving it for other educators that are struggling with it too. That's how you're going to create a thriving, successful online business!

Today you will Show Out by creating a social media post to share the one problem that your online business will help educators solve. Don't forget to tag me @ericaterryceo on Instagram and use the hashtag #ClassroomtoCEOin30days so that I can show your post some love. If you're not quite comfortable with sharing that with the world just yet, leave a comment inside of the companion course so that I know you made your Success Move today. I can show you some love there too!

DAY 7
WHO'S YOUR FAVORITE EDUCATOR?

Tell me a story about your Favorite Educator.

I'm willing to bet that right now, your mind is going back to a special moment during your childhood when a teacher, counselor, or administrator made a significant difference in your life.

I have so many wonderful memories from my Favorite Educators. From my seventh-grade science teacher, Ms. Latrice Bradford, rewarding us with a trip to Red Lobster (which was a big deal back in that day) to my eighth-grade science teacher, Mrs. Robin Norwood, being courageous enough to have honest, real talks with her hormonal, adolescent, ask waaayyy too many personal questions students to my ninth-grade French teacher, Ms. Jeanne Lee, who poured so much love and care into her students that no matter what was happening around you, when you walked out of her room, you felt like you could conquer the world.

Does your Favorite Educator story sound familiar? Does it bring to remembrance great memories that you'll cherish forever?

I'm sure that it does because until today, anytime you heard the term "Favorite Teacher" or, in this case, "Favorite Educator," your mind immediately went to whoever left the greatest mark on your life. This educator was able to reach you in a way that no one else could. When you've imagined the impact that you want to make in the lives of your students, you've looked to that educator as your example of how students should feel when they're in your presence.

Remember last week when we discussed the need to transition from your educator mindset to an edupreneur mindset? Well, here's another area where you must transform your mindset to achieve success. As an edupreneur, your Favorite Educator isn't the one that made the greatest impact in your life, but rather the one whose life you can have the greatest impact on.

From this moment on, your Favorite Educator is the one who looks to you as an example of how students should be made to feel. It's the one that's struggling with the main problem that your online business solves to such a degree that she grabs every product that you create because it's helping her to transform her practices to become the educator that she always imagined she would be.

When deciding which product to create next, it's going to be important for you to always have your Favorite Educator in mind because she's the one that you're creating products for.

To ensure that your products are meeting her needs and truly helping her to transform her practices so that she can have the positive impact that she always imagined she would have, you must decipher everything about her. Or, in other words, you have to get all up in her business. ALL. UP. IN. IT. Otherwise, you won't truly be able to impact her in a way that changes her life.

So I'm going to ask you again…

Who's your Favorite Educator?

It's important for you to answer this question thoroughly because it's going to be knowing this person inside and out that's going to be the determining factor between a side hustle that earns coffee money and one that earns comma money.

Just in case you've never listened to the Classroom to CEO Podcast, you may be unfamiliar with the difference between coffee money and comma money so allow me to explain...

When your side hustle consists mainly of selling $2 digital resources, then the outcome is coffee money. You earn enough money to buy a cup of coffee every day, but not much more. On the other hand, when your side hustle consists of creating and earning revenue from multiple streams of income, you will begin to earn comma money. When the amount being deposited into your business bank account every month requires a comma (i.e.,. $1,000+), then you're officially earning #CommaMoney.

Now that you understand the difference between coffee money and #CommaMoney, let's get back to the question that I asked earlier.

Who's your Favorite Educator?

At this point, I can hear you saying, "Erica, I'd love to answer that question, but I'm starting an online business that helps students, so I can't."

If you're starting a business that helps students, then create a profile for your Favorite Student. Keep in mind that your Favorite Student is the one that your business will focus on helping to overcome his #StudentProblems and not the characteristics of the most well-behaved student in your class.

The same is true if you're working with school psychologists, social workers, school counselors, paraprofessionals, or other educators that have a role outside of the classroom. Rather than your Favorite

Educator, replace this terminology with your Favorite _____, and answer the question accordingly.

Now that we've cleared that up, let me clarify one more point…

Moving from the Classroom to CEO is going to require you to do much more than create a bunch of random, no-prep resources that teachers can easily print off and give to students when they don't feel like planning their own lessons. This approach may have allowed teachers to build profitable online businesses a few years ago, but those days are behind us. I hate to break it to you, but you've missed that boat.

In 2020 and beyond, to make your edupreneur dreams come true requires you to create life-changing products that empower educators to transform their practices and create a life that they love waking up to on Monday mornings. To create at this level, you have to know exactly what your customer (i.e., Favorite Educator) needs, and you won't know that unless you know everything about them, including who they are from the inside and out.

CEO Success Move #7:
Who is Your Favorite Educator?

During today's CEO Success Move, you will view the video inside of Day 7 of the companion course where I describe exactly how to outline the characteristics of your Favorite Educator. Remember that your Favorite Educator is the one who is struggling the most with the problem that your online business solves.

YOU SHOWED UP.

NOW IT'S TIME TO SHOW OUT!

Who is your Favorite Educator?

Seriously, I really want to know.

Create a social media post where you give a shout-out to someone that exemplifies the characteristics that you outlined as your Favorite Educator. Tell that person something that you admire about them. Remember, she may one day be a member of your online community, so be kind.

As always, tag me @ericaterryceo on Instagram and use the hashtag #ClassroomtoCEOin30days so that I can show your post and your Favorite Educator some love. I'm super excited to meet educators from around the world, so don't forget to tag me!

DAY 8
CRAFT A STORY THAT SELLS

I recall during my first year as a high school Biology teacher, I found it very difficult to navigate the growing pains of co-teaching. Every day I felt overwhelmed as I attempted to deal with misbehaviors that I'd never encountered during student teaching and, to be honest, that I wasn't prepared to deal with. All this while taking on the majority of the instruction as well as spending every evening and weekend planning lessons and grading papers.

Talk about stress, frustration, and overwhelm…

I was on the fast track to teacher burnout, so much so that every school break, winter, spring, AND summer, my body shut down, causing me to spend the majority of it lying in bed sick.

The stress and frustration felt like a ton of bricks on my shoulders. There were times when I felt that it was waaayyyy too much for me to handle.

It didn't help matters much that at the same time, I had to work a second job at Dillard's so that I could supplement my measly $35K salary (Yep! $35,000/year was my first-year salary **with** a master's *degree). Although it was over 15 years ago, as I write these words, the very thought of that entire first-year experience is making me feel stressed out all over again.*

BUT GOD! (*raising both hands in the air & doing a praise dance)

That was 2003. Fast forward to 2021, and not only have I been able to successfully use my #EducatorProblem to secure a book deal that will empower co-teachers all over the world to transform instruction to meet the needs of ALL students, but through the Classroom to CEO Podcast, I get to spend my time doing something that I absolutely love—empowering educators to use their knowledge and expertise to turn their #EducatorProblems into a profitable online business too!

Won't He do it?

The story that you just read is a snippet of the full story that I share with educators when I speak and consult. I'm real, raw, and completely transparent about my experiences as an educator because I never know what someone is really going through or the adversity that they're faced with.

When sharing my story, my goal is to always let people know that they are not alone and that no matter what #EducatorProblems they're going through, when they make the shift to an edupreneur mindset, there's a life that they love waiting on the other side.

I'm willing to share the good, bad, and the ugly, if that's what it takes to empower even one educator to change their life. Personally, I'm completely comfortable with sharing the details of my #EducatorProblem stories, but you may not be, and that's ok too.

While you don't have to openly share ALL of the details of your story, I highly recommend that you find a few intimate parts that you're willing to share. Then, share them often and with everyone who's willing to listen.

Right now, at this very moment, your Favorite Educator is struggling with her #EducatorProblems. She's dealing with stress, overwhelm, and frustration like never before and do you know the one thing she needs from you more than anything else?

She needs this one thing more than your online course.

She needs this one thing more than any digital resources that you create.

She needs this one thing more than the coaching and consulting services that you'll offer.

The one thing that your Favorite Educator needs from you more than anything else is hope.

An educator that is struggling needs to know that there is peace on the other side of the situation that's stressing her out.

The best way for you to provide the hope that she so desperately needs is by being transparent enough to share intimate details about how you once struggled with the same #EducatorProblem that she now faces. While doing so, be honest and share the raw truth about what you had to go through in order to get to the other side. Give her hope that one day she will experience the peace and joy that's on the other side of her #EducatorProblems. This is what I like to call your #EducatorProblem Story.

Typically when educators talk about their #EducatorProblems, they spend the majority of their time complaining about the challenges that they face. They don't share their story to help anyone else. Instead, they share it as an opportunity to vent and release their frustrations. They talk about their #EducatorProblems to help themselves. An educator that's focused on helping themself is clearly not operating with an edupreneur mindset.

When you're operating with an educator mindset, your #EducatorProblems = Opportunity to Get Empathy from Others

The opposite is true when you're operating with an edupreneur mindset.

When you're focused on moving from the Classroom to CEO and achieving success as an edupreneur, suddenly your #EducatorProblems become an opportunity to empower others. It's no longer about the pain and stress that you're experiencing; it's about how you can help other educators reduce the pain and stress that they're experiencing.

When you're operating with an edupreneur mindset, your #EducatorProblems = Opportunity to Empower and Inspire Others

As a successful edupreneur, when you share your #EducatorProblem Story, you're not doing so to get empathy for yourself, but to empower others. You're not sharing your #EducatorProblem Story to vent, but rather to inspire.

As you craft your #EducatorProblem Story, it's important to understand that after you provide educators with the inspiration and hope they need to begin believing that it is possible for them to have a much more positive and rewarding experience, your work isn't done. Sharing your #EducatorProblem Story is the easy part.

The next part of your #EducatorProblem Story is where it gets hard because take my word for it… It's easy to inspire, but it's hard to convince people to take action and make a change. How does the saying go? *You can lead a horse to the water, but you can't make them drink it.* Well, to be a successful edupreneur, your job is to lead them to the water AND make them drink it.

When crafting an #EducatorProblem Story that sells your product for you, which, if you haven't guessed by now, is what you'll be doing during today's CEO Success Move, you have to do more than share WHAT you did; you must also share HOW you did it.

The second part of your #EducatorProblem Story must include tips and strategies that your Favorite Educator can implement to achieve the goal of overcoming their #EducatorProblem.

It's sharing the HOW that transforms your #EducatorProblem Story from a story of inspiration and hope to one that actually empowers other educators to take action and transform their lives.

Are you ready to craft a Powerful #EducatorProblem Story that allows you to empower educators all over the world?

Awesome! Let's do this!

CEO Success Move #8:
Craft a Powerful #EducatorProblem Story
that sells your product for you.

For your CEO Success Move today, you are going to write the first draft of your #EducatorProblem Story. It's the first draft because as you further reminisce about your experiences and continue to work daily to build a profitable online business, you will recall more and more details that you can always come back and add to your story later. Today you will get the story started.

Inside of Day 8 of the companion course, you will get a chance to hear the #EducatorProblem Story that I share when I teach principles of edupreneurship, as well as tips to help you complete today's success move. While I can't write the story for you, I can provide some useful tips along the way. Be sure to check them out, especially if you find yourself struggling while trying to make this Success Move.

YOU SHOWED UP.
NOW IT'S TIME TO SHOW OUT!

Congratulations on creating the first draft of your #EducatorProblem Story! While you may not be ready to share it publicly just yet, I encourage you to make a video of yourself sharing your story. It's important that you get used to hearing yourself tell the story because you're going to be sharing it A LOT!

If you feel comfortable sharing your story and using it to promote your future business, by all means, do it and make sure that you tag me @ericaterryceo on Instagram + use the hashtag #ClassroomtoCEOin30days so that I can show your post some love.

If you're not quite yet comfortable sharing your #EducatorProblem Story, that's ok too! Find a quote that expresses how your story makes you feel or the joy you feel now that you're on the other side of it. Once again, be sure to tag me @ericaterryceo on Instagram + use the hashtag #ClassroomtoCEOin30days.

DAY 9
CEO EMPOWERMENT STATEMENT

W hen I was in high school, my friends and I would sit at the cafeteria table talking about the latest episode of *A Different World* or laughing at how funny *Martin* was that week. Some of us grew up with mothers that watched soap operas, so we'd spend time discussing the latest ploy of Victor Newnan or trying to guess how his ongoing rivalry with Jack Abbot would play out on *The Young and the Restless*.

No matter if we were laughing and joking at *Martin* or trying to guess who the father was of the latest secret child on *The Young and the Restless*, all the while, I was carrying a secret that I was too embarrassed to tell anyone about.

Every day at 2:50 PM when the final bell rang, it wasn't Victor Newnan, Jack Abbott, Nikki, or Neil that made me run home and turn on the TV. The characters on TV that I was totally obsessed with were named Jean, Storm, Professor X, and Wolverine. *The Young and the Restless* was good, but *X-Men* was great! My obsession with the *X-Men* cartoon was the deep, dark secret that I harbored throughout high school. I mean, I was in high school, for goodness sake, and I didn't think that any of my friends would understand why I was so captivated by *X-Men*.

Truth be told, *X-Men* was my favorite show ever! It was a cartoon, but the relationships, combined with the complexities of being superheroes, made for good TV. It helped me understand that even though they were mutants born with great superpowers, they each still dealt with their own share of issues. Storms' ability to control weather didn't mean that her claustrophobia didn't cause her to panic at the worst possible moment.

Years later, I'd realize that it wasn't just Storm, Jean, and Professor X that had to deal with issues despite the fact that they had superpowers. Every educator that must use their superpowers daily to ensure that they are positively impacting the lives of students while also dealing with their own share of struggles is a superhero.

You, my friend, are a superhero, and today you are going to identify a superpower and describe how you will use it for good by crafting a CEO Empowerment Statement.

Taking the time to clarify your message is important to your ability to achieve success as an edupreneur. If there's one lesson that I learned during my years in the classroom that I've taken with me into the online business world, it is the fact that when students are confused, they don't commit. They don't commit to paying attention throughout the lesson, and they don't commit to getting the work done.

But when the lightbulb goes off, and they experience that 'aha' moment, everything changes. All of a sudden they're ready to do the work because they understand what they're doing. The more clarity and insight they gain into a topic, the more they ask questions and engage in the lesson. When there's clarity, students commit to paying attention throughout the lesson and they commit to getting the work done.

This same principle applies to business. Customers that are confused don't commit.

They don't commit to engaging in your online community because they don't understand what you do.

They don't commit to engaging with you on social media because they don't understand what you're trying to say.

They don't commit to buying your products because they don't understand how what you're selling fits their needs.

CONFUSION ≠ COMMITMENT

But when you have a clear message that helps other educators make the connection about how your superpower can help them, they experience that 'aha' moment. When that happens, just like we see in students, everything changes. All of a sudden, when you send an email and ask a question at the end, people take the time to respond back. When you create a social media post, it gets likes and comments because your followers understand the message that you're sending. When you introduce a new product, they buy it because they understand how it helps them.

CLARITY = COMMITMENT

When you're starting an online business, one of the most important steps is to clarify your message so that people instantly connect with you and the brand that you are creating.

Now don't get it twisted. Many people skip this step because crafting a message that invokes enough emotion to make someone feel instantly connected to your brand is no easy task, but it is a necessary one.

Your messaging must be so clear and concise that it literally stops someone dead in their tracks.

It stops them from moving that finger that's making their screen scroll down through their social media feed.

It stops their eyes from continuing to move down the Google search feed.

Why is it important to make them stop scrolling? Simply because when they stop scrolling, they click.

They click to visit your website.

They click to learn more about you.

They click to read your latest post.

They click to learn more about your products.

They click to buy.

CLARITY = CLICKS

But if they find themselves confused, then guess what they do next. Yep, you guessed it. They click off.

CONFUSION = CLICK OFF

I don't want people clicking off shortly after they begin to interact with your brand, which is why today, your CEO Success Move is to craft a clear, concise CEO Empowerment Statement.

Your CEO Empowerment Statement is not going to be a long, drawn-out paragraph that explains your mission and tells the world everything about you, including your why.

No! No! No! Remember, our number one golden rule is to always keep it SIMPLE!!!

So the CEO Empowerment Statement that you create today is going to be ONE sentence that clearly communicates the purpose of your online business.

You're going to tell people what you do and who you do it for. It's as simple as filling in the blanks to this statement:

I Empower _____ to _____.

Here are a couple of the CEO Empowerment Statements that I use:

- I empower educators to start a side hustle and create multiple streams of income.
- I empower co-teachers to develop collaborative relationships and transform instruction to meet the needs of ALL students.

Let me be clear. Your CEO Empowerment Statement Is ONLY ONE SENTENCE. (*Yes, the Power of One applies here too.*)

It's a powerful sentence that attracts attention and makes people click to learn more. When they click, that's when you give them all the details. For today, focus only on catching their attention.

CEO Success Move #9:

Craft Your CEO Empowerment Statement

During today's CEO Success Move, you will craft your CEO Empowerment Statement.

If you're feeling stuck while crafting your CEO Empowerment Statement, take a look at the examples that are included in the companion course, and just know that your statement will never be perfect. It will continue to evolve and change as you grow as an edupreneur. Believe me when I tell you that I'm constantly tweaking my CEO Empowerment Statement.

After you finish your CEO Empowerment Statement, be sure to come back here so that you can Show Out and share with me how you will empower other educators to achieve success.

YOU SHOWED UP.

NOW IT'S TIME TO SHOW OUT!

Congratulations on crafting your CEO Empowerment Statement! I am so very proud of you for showing up and doing the work!

Now that you can clearly communicate how your superpower will help educators achieve success, it's time to share it with the world. Create a social media post that shares your CEO Empowerment Statement and tag me @ericaterryceo on Instagram + use the hashtag #ClassroomtoCEOin30days so that I can show your post some love.

DAY 10
DROP THE MIC NAME

Have you ever been in a store minding your own business, and all of a sudden, someone walks past you, and you stop dead in your tracks because you notice that they have on the cutest shoes?

Ok... maybe that's just me because I'm a shoe fanatic, but when I see someone with a pair of cute shoes on, I immediately stop that person and say something like, "OMG! I love those shoes. What store did you buy them from?"

Sometimes the person can point me to the right place so that I can grab a pair, but then there are those times that the person replies, "Thanks, but I honestly don't remember."

If there are three words that can kill your ability to achieve success as an edupreneur, it's "I don't remember."

You can create the greatest products in the world, but if an educator goes to talk about how much your product helped them and they can't remember your name, that will instantly kill any hope of you achieving a level of success that allows you to reach your goal of moving from the Classroom to CEO.

If I had a penny for every time I've sat in meetings with educators and engaged in a conversation where someone says something like, "Does anyone know of a good program that will help me manage the behavior issues in my classroom?" Another person replies by sharing information from a presentation that they attended, and when they're asked about the name of the program, they say, "I don't remember."

Can you guess what happens next?

Those three words, *I don't remember*, lead to a Google search, which then leads to a program which nine times out of ten wasn't the one that the person learned about in the presentation.

The result is that the edupreneur that invested in the travel and fees associated with presenting at a conference lost a possible sale because even though the conference participants were thoroughly impressed with the product (enough so that they could remember details about it months later and refer it to someone else), they couldn't remember the product name so they were unsuccessful in their attempt to recommend it to someone else.

How different would this story be if the name was memorable?

When asked the name of the program, they would say, "Oh, it was called Super Duper SEL Strategies." The person that needed behavior management strategies would perform a Google search for Super Duper SEL strategies and guess what comes up.... www.superdupersel.com. They click the link and go directly to the website of the edupreneur that made the presentation at the conference, and they purchase the product, and the rest is history.

Most edupreneurs that I meet invest hours to ensure that every product and service that they create is perfect. They make sure that every "i" is dotted and every "t" is crossed. When they venture out and begin growing their business by presenting at conferences and appearing on podcasts, they invest hours crafting an amazing message that inspires and empowers other educators to achieve success.

They've got all of those essential parts down to a science, but one area that they fail to invest their time in is crafting the perfect name for their online business, and as you can see, NAMES MATTER!

The quality of the products that you create will help you turn the educator that's using it into a paying customer, but it's your name that turns that one paying customer into a lot more. When you have a memorable name, it makes it easier for customers to recommend you to others, and that's when your business grows.

1 great product **without** a great name = 1 customer
1 great product **with** a great name = unlimited customers

Your name is just as important as the quality of the products that you'll begin to create in a few days. That's why for today's CEO Success Move, you're going to spend time crafting the perfect name for your online business.

What makes a name perfect? I'm so glad you asked!

The perfect name for your online business not only speaks to the problem that you help educators to solve, but it is also memorable while being flashy enough to make people stop dead in their tracks as if you have on the cutest pair of shoes in the world.

The perfect name for your online business that you will come up with today is going to lead to a Drop the MIC Moment.

At this point, you may be asking yourself, "How can a name result in a Drop the Mic Moment?" Well, let me tell you!

As I'm writing this, I can already see your future. The online business that you're creating during our 30 days together is going to have such an amazing impact on the lives of others that it's going to open doors for you to present at conferences and get on stages all over the world. You're going to be invited to give presentations, provide professional development in schools, and deliver the keynote at your favorite educational conference.

When you do, someone is going to introduce and welcome you to the stage as "Your Name, founder of Your Online Business Name."

When you're announced, I want your name to be so strong that you don't have to say another word. You can walk on the stage and drop the mic because everyone already knows who you're there to help and what you're going to help them do simply because they heard your name.

To craft your perfect, Drop the MIC Name it must contain all three of these essential elements:

1. **M**emorable
2. **I**dentifies the Problem or Solution
3. **C**asts a Vision of the Future

Memorable

I can pretty much guarantee that educators are going to absolutely LOVE the products that you will create using the FAST Freebie & Product Creation Method. Your online business is going to empower them beyond belief to overcome a problem that they've been struggling with, so naturally, they are going to talk about their success with other educators.

When they begin to talk about the unbelievable results that they've been able to achieve, your goal is to ensure that they remember who it was that they got the product from, so that they can refer their educator friends directly to your online store.

If you create products that help teachers effectively manage disruptive behaviors in their classroom, you don't want them to have to do a generic search on social-emotional strategies, because then they'll encounter hundreds of other teacher sellers that create resources about this same issue.

Instead, you want them to lead people straight to your online business, and to do so, they must remember your name!

Memorable business names are not just catchy, but they are also simple and easy to spell. You don't want to confuse people by turning an "s" into "z" like in "School Dayz" versus "School Days" or using the number "2" instead of "to" like in "Classroom 2 CEO" vs. "Classroom to CEO."

When it comes to naming, always KEEP IT SIMPLE!

Identifies the Problem and/or Solution

We live in a scroll, scroll, click world. What this means for you is that your business name must not only be memorable, but as someone is scrolling through their newsfeed, it has to make them stop dead in their tracks. They have to stop scrolling long enough to actually read and learn about what you're offering.

The only way to guarantee that they stop scrolling is by crafting a name that specifically addresses a problem that they've been struggling with, or provides the solution that they've been looking for.

Casts a Vision of the Future

When a brand name communicates to someone a snapshot of what their future can look like, magic happens. All of a sudden, your brand becomes about them. When someone reads my name, Classroom to CEO, they aren't thinking about me. They're not wondering how I made it from the Classroom to CEO. They think about themselves and the future that's possible for them.

The best part is that even if they've never thought about owning their own business and becoming a CEO, it creates curiosity and causes them to imagine a future that they may not have thought was possible.

Classroom to CEO encompasses all three essential elements of the Drop the MIC Name Formula.

It's memorable by being short and easy to spell.

While it doesn't directly state the problem, if you are a frustrated, stressed out, and overwhelmed teacher, as soon as you read the word "Classroom," you immediately begin to imagine the #EducatorProblems that have you stressed out in that particular moment. As you're envisioning those #EducatorProblems, all of a sudden you keep reading, and BAM, there's the solution, "CEO."

Suddenly you're no longer focused on your #EducatorProblems, but you're beginning to imagine your prosperous future.

And the best part is that you've experienced that full range of emotions before I even say, "Hi! My name is Erica Terry, and I'm the founder of Classroom to CEO."

MIC DROPS

Now it's your turn to Drop the MIC!

> # CEO Success Move #10:
> ### Craft a Drop the MIC name
> ### for your online business.

During today's CEO Success Move, you are going to begin the process of crafting your Drop the MIC Name. Before we begin, let me be 100% honest with you. The likelihood that you'll walk away today with your Drop the MIC Name is slim. Crafting the perfect name is HARD WORK, but just know that it's ok if you don't come up with one today.

Think of this process as a marathon rather than a 100-meter dash. Once you begin to generate ideas and solicit feedback, you'll find yourself in the middle of doing something totally unrelated to your business, like working out or even right in the middle of teaching a lesson, and out of nowhere, the perfect Drop the MIC name will pop into your head. As soon as it does, you're going to say, 'That's It!"

Once you have selected your Drop the Mic name, I recommend that you go ahead and create social media profiles/pages for your business. We will discuss how to effectively use social media in your business on Day 27, but go ahead and grab the username now before someone else does!

YOU SHOWED UP.

NOW IT'S TIME TO SHOW OUT!

Congratulations on crafting your Drop the MIC Name! I am so very proud of you for showing up and doing the work!

Now that you have your Drop the MIC Name, it's time to share it with the world. Create a social media post that shares your Drop the MIC Name and tag me @ericaterryceo on Instagram + use the hashtag #ClassroomtoCEOin30days so that I can show your post some love.

If you started a social media account with your Drop the MIC name, you could also create a *coming soon* post to let people know that it's on the way.

STEP 3 | MAKE A CEO
SUCCESS PLAN

DAY 11
CEO SUCCESS PLAN

Nothing gets my creative juices flowing more than creating a Drop the MIC Name. Once I have the name, my mind suddenly begins to fill up with product ideas.

If you're anything like me, when you think of all the great ideas that you have, you envision yourself empowering educators all over the world to achieve success. Not only that, but let's be honest. You also envision yourself earning millions in no time.

Ok… maybe you're not at the point of dreaming of earning millions of dollars as an edupreneur, but you do believe that the ideas floating through your head are going to allow you to earn more than your current salary and help you move from the Classroom to CEO.

The biggest challenge that you're faced with right now isn't a lack of ideas, but rather deciding which idea you should begin to develop first.

Or the complete opposite may be true.

You may have looked at the size of the #EducatorProblem that you selected and said to yourself, "How in the world am I supposed to empower educators to solve this?"

The challenge that you're faced with right now is figuring out a product that isn't so big that the very thought of it scares you into believing that you'll never get it finished. You, too, are struggling to identify where to begin, but for an entirely different reason.

Believe it or not, no matter if you have millions of ideas floating around your head or if the one idea that you have is so big that it seems impossible, you're actually in the same exact spot because guess what…

Your ideas are worth nothing until you've organized them in a way that makes sense and truly empowers your Favorite Educator to achieve success by overcoming her #EducatorProblems.

If you make the mistake of trying to build an online business where you convert a bunch of your lesson plans into digital resources, a couple of months from now, you will find yourself caught up in a vicious cycle of trying to create 100+ digital resources to add to a store that no one is shopping from.

I can't emphasize enough that the strategy of turning your lessons into digital resources and selling them from a teacher marketplace will not result in your success as an edupreneur. Instead, you will find yourself stressed out and overwhelmed, while barely earning enough money from your side hustle to support your coffee habit, let alone make your edupreneur vision of success into a reality.

Maybe converting lesson plans wasn't your plan. Maybe you've caught on to the idea of creating multiple streams of income and decided that you are going to quickly grow your side hustle income by selling digital resources, teaching online courses, hosting a membership group, and starting a podcast all at the same time.

Raise your hand if that's what you've been thinking about doing.

Ok, I see you.

Well, take it from me; that strategy doesn't work either. Much like the vicious 100+ digital resource cycle, you will find yourself creating a bunch of products that no one will buy and guess where that will leave you. Yep! Earning coffee money instead of comma money.

Trust me when I tell you that strategy doesn't work either. I would know because I have attempted to create every product on the market. I've been all over the place in my product creation process. I've tried to create online courses, printable resources, a membership group.... The list goes on and on.

When it comes to product creation, you name it, I've tried it!

At the beginning of my journey, I wasted a lot of time, energy, and money trying to figure this whole online business, how to be a successful edupreneur thing out. Worst of all, for much of the time that I was figuring it out, I was calling myself an edupreneur, but yet I wasn't earning any money.

Before I discovered the value of creating a CEO Success Plan, before creating products, my product creation and launch formula looked something like this:

- An idea would pop into my head.
- I'd spend a few weeks on Google researching the idea and figuring out the most cost-efficient way to make it happen.
- I'd spend the next few weeks (or months) creating the product myself because I certainly wasn't going to pay someone else to create it.

- When the product was finished, with high hopes and no strategy, I'd launch it the world…
- And what I found waiting on the other side of my product launch was crickets.
- After no one bought my new product, I would end up feeling defeated. I had just spent the last few months working my tail off to turn my great idea into a product, and at the end of it all, I still wasn't earning enough money to cover the costs of running an online business, and I was nowhere near making my dreams come true.

Talk about stress, frustration, and despair. I was over it!

That was my experience as an edupreneur, until the day that I discovered the value of mapping out a CEO Success Plan, **before** deciding which freebies and products to create. Doing so ensures that all of the products that I create align with my CEO Empowerment Statement and ultimately achieve the goal of empowering my Favorite Educator to overcome her #EducatorProblems.

Creating a CEO Success Plan before I create a product allows me to take my customers on a journey that makes sense and empowers them to reach their goals. It also allows me to earn money from multiple revenue sources seamlessly.

My CEO Success Plan for the educational consulting that I do around co-teaching looks something like this:

- **CEO Empowerment Statement:** I help co-teachers develop strong collaborative relationships and transform instruction to meet the needs of ALL students.
- **Choose ONE Problem:** Co-teachers struggle to foster collaborative relationships that result in shared planning and teaching
- **Address the most common complaint:** Co-Teachers don't

have time to co-plan. The general education teacher complains of feeling stressed out and overwhelmed by having to do all of the planning and teaching. The special education teacher feels left out and more like an assistant than a certified professional.

- **Simple Step-by-Step Solution:** 5 step co-planning framework that can be implemented in a virtual environment even if the teachers don't have a common co-planning time
- **Turn one small part into a Solution-Focused Freebie:** Digital resource, which is a template that includes the 5 steps of the co-planning framework. This freebie is a simple one-pager that shares WHAT to do during co-planning time.
- **Solution-Focused Product:** Digital toolkit that includes multiple resources that share HOW to implement each step of the co-planning framework either face-to-face or in a virtual environment.
- **Additional Income Stream:** Co-Teaching Virtual Coaching Program: Consists of mini-professional learning sessions followed by opportunities for me to observe and provide feedback to both co-teachers.

See how that works?

One free resource leads to a low-cost digital toolkit, which leads to a coaching program that costs more and allows me to earn revenue from different income sources.

Right now, you have a choice to make.

You can build your online business by converting a bunch of lesson plans into digital products, and a few months from now, find yourself earning coffee money while being stuck in the cycle of trying to create 100+ digital resources to add to your online store.

-or-

You can build your business using the SIMPLE Classroom to CEO in 30 Days System, which starts by creating a CEO Success Plan that will enable you to create and earn money from multiple sources within the next few months.

If you choose to go the SIMPLE Classroom to CEO in 30 Days route, you will discover that when you create resources AFTER creating your CEO Success Plan, everything flows together much more smoothly. What ends up happening is that not only do you create a freebie, but you also have an action plan to create additional products that educators will need to completely overcome the problem that you are helping them to solve.

The SIMPLE Classroom to CEO in 30 Days System eliminates the need to create 100 random resources that you sell for $2-$3 because every product you create leads to the next more expensive product in your CEO Success Plan. It also eliminates the process of creating a bunch of different online courses or, even worse, one humongous course that doesn't help anyone.

The CEO Success Plan streamlines the process so that you always stay focused on the ultimate goal of empowering your Favorite Educator to overcome their #EducatorProblem.

If you haven't guessed by now, today's CEO Success Move requires you to begin the process of creating your first CEO Success Plan. We will start working on it today, and then you will spend the next week planning and working out all of the specific details.

Creating a CEO Success Plan empowers you to create amazing products that are aligned with your CEO Empowerment Statement and ultimately lead to your Favorite Educator being able to achieve success.

As your online business grows, you will continue to create additional CEO Success Plans, and over time they will become much more complex. On Day 30, you will launch an online business that includes a freebie and one product. As your business grows and you continue to engage in the Classroom to CEO community, you will learn how to turn that main product into additional products and services that allow you to earn money from your side hustle by creating multiple streams of income.

CEO Success Move #11:

Begin Creating a CEO Success Plan

During today's CEO Success Move, you will begin drafting your CEO Success Plan. Throughout this week, we will continue to outline your success plan and then use it to create your first freebie and product together.

YOU SHOWED UP.

NOW IT'S TIME TO SHOW OUT!

To achieve success, you have to move past your fears and confidently put yourself out there as an edupreneur. Today you will create a social media post to let your friends, family, and teacher friends know that your online business is *coming soon*. You will also let them know the specific problem that you will be helping educators to solve. Tag me @ericaterryceo on Instagram + use the hashtag #ClassroomtoCEOin30days so that I can show your post some love.

DAY 12
KEEP IT SIMPLE!

One of the keys to achieving success as an edupreneur comes in knowing which practices from the classroom suit you well as an edupreneur and which practices you need to completely get rid of. One practice that you perfect in the classroom that is essential to edupreneur success is the ability to break down complex problems into bite-sized pieces that make it easy for students to understand.

As a high school Biology teacher, I often found myself breaking down vocabulary and scientific processes in a way that ninth-graders could easily understand. I'm willing to bet that in your experience as an educator, you've had to do the same countless times.

Your ability to break down complex topics so that everyone can master them is a skill that will serve you well as an edupreneur. When it comes to the ONE problem that your online business solves, you are going to have to lean on that skill again.

Today you will be asked to create a simple, step-by-step solution to your #EducatorProblem.

Oh no. There goes that word again.

Simple...

First, I asked you to begin implementing 6 SIMPLE Steps to move from the Classroom to CEO in 30 Days, and now here I am asking you to create a simple solution to your #EducatorProblem. Are you tired of me yet? I hope not because we're just getting this party started!

On Day 7, you outlined the barriers and challenges that your Favorite Educator is experiencing. You, too, probably experienced many of those same #EducatorProblems, which is why you were so easily able to describe them as you crafted your #EducatorProblem Story on Day 8.

Now it's time to turn your experiences into a solution that you will eventually use to help other educators overcome their problems. For you to truly help your Favorite Educator achieve success, you must turn the strategies that you've used into a simple, step-by-step solution that can be easily implemented.

Oftentimes when you're good at something, you take it for granted. You don't understand why other teachers have trouble reaching Jimmy because when he enters your classroom, the student they describe is not the one that you see. You've been able to develop a great student-teacher relationship with him even though no one else in your building has been able to get close to him at all.

The strategies that you use feel so natural to you that you don't think twice about what you're doing. You just do it! If you're shaking your head up and down because you know exactly what I'm talking about, the challenge that you're faced with today is having to figure out exactly what it is that you're doing or have done to overcome that #EducatorProblem and outlining exact steps that others can implement.

Even if the solution really isn't that simple, your job is to break it down in a way that makes people believe that it is. Often when I begin working with co-teachers, their past experiences have been so negative that they don't believe that it's possible to develop a strong, collaborative relationship. They also don't believe that they'll be able to co-plan engaging lessons that meet the needs of ALL students. Combine this with barriers such as working virtually or not having a shared planning period, and you'll understand why it's so important to utilize this skill as an edupreneur.

As a CEO, you must empower your Favorite Educator to shift their mindset and believe in the possibilities that lie ahead. To do so, provide a simple solution that empowers educators to overcome their problems and achieve success.

CEO Success Move #12:

Create a Simple, Step-by-Step Solution

Your CEO Success Move for today is to create a simple, step-by-step solution that you will add to the CEO Success Plan that you started yesterday. The goal of this solution is to help teachers overcome the #EducatorProblem that you chose on Day 6.

YOU SHOWED UP.

NOW IT'S TIME TO SHOW OUT!

Create a social media post sharing a memory that you have from when you were struggling with the #EducatorProblem that you created a solution for today. This post will serve as a teaser for your upcoming freebie as well as an opportunity to begin establishing positive relationships with your Favorite Educators.

Like yesterday, make the post fun and engaging so that it builds excitement, and then tag me @ericaterryceo on Instagram + use the hashtag #ClassroomtoCEOin30days so that I can show your post some love.

DAY 13
SIMPLE FAST STARS, JUST TO NAME A FEW

Please Excuse My Dear Aunt Sally...

A ny idea of what that means?
How about these?

King Phillip Came Over From Great Spain...
King Henry Died Drinking Chocolate Milk

Ok... Maybe you haven't taught any of these popular phrases in your classroom so let me toss out some words that you may recognize.

HOMES
PEMDAS

No to the words? How about this name?

ROY G BIV

At this point, if you're still not sure why I'm over here throwing all of these random phrases out at you, let me explain.

Depending on the grade level and/or subject that you teach, you may have recognized those as popular mnemonic devices and acronyms that many teachers use to help their students remember important concepts. For example, *Please Excuse My Dear Aunt Sally* and *PEMDAS* are used to teach the Order of Operations (Parenthesis, Exponents, Multiplication, Division, Addition, Subtraction).

Just like mnemonic devices and acronyms are great tools to help students remember, the same principle applies when working with your Favorite Educators. Turning the step-by-step solution that you developed yesterday into a mnemonic device or acronym makes it easier for your Favorite Educator to constantly keep it in mind so that they can easily assess where they are as they are putting the strategies that they teach into action.

As you continue to engage in the Classroom to CEO community, you will discover acronyms everywhere. This entire book is based on the SIMPLE 6 step Classroom to CEO in 30 Days System that I developed to empower educators, just like you, to turn their knowledge and expertise into a profitable online business. If you skipped the introduction, then you may not have realized that SIMPLE is an acronym that stands for each of the 6 steps in the solution that I created to help educators to move from the Classroom to CEO. Those steps are:

Step 1| Shift to a Successful Edupreneur Mindset
Step 2| Identify One Problem to Solve
Step 3| Make a CEO Success Plan
Step 4| Produce a Solution-Focused Freebie + Product
Step 5| List Build Like PROS
Step 6| Engage as an Expert

Then there's the Drop the MIC Name formula that I shared with you on Day 10. Just in case you forgot, MIC is an acronym that describes the three essential elements of a business or product name:

- **M**emorable
- **I**dentifies the Problem or Solution
- **C**asts a Vision of the Future

It doesn't stop there. Before this 30-day journey is over, there will be a couple of more acronyms that you'll put into practice, so keep your eyes open.

The reason why I use so many acronyms in my business is due to the simple fact that they work. Just like they work to help students recall important information, they work for educators too!

I've turned my solutions into an easy to remember acronym, and now it's your turn to do the same. Ready to make today's CEO Success Move? Let's do it!

CEO Success Move #13:
Create an Acronym or Mnemonic Device to
represent your Step-by-Step Solution.

During today's CEO Success Move, you will create an easy-to-remember acronym or mnemonic device using the simple, step-by-step solution that you developed yesterday in Success Move #12. While you're not going to change the outcome of each step, you may have to change a few of the words to accomplish this task.

Feeling stuck? Use thesaurus.com. Trust me, it will be your best friend today. Also, check out Day 13 of the companion course for additional examples of acronyms that I've used.

YOU SHOWED UP.

NOW IT'S TIME TO SHOW OUT!

I'm willing to bet that the acronym you created today is amazing; therefore, I'm not going to ask you to put it out into the world just yet.

Instead, you will create a social media post sharing a strategy related to your #EducatorProblem, that you've used to help others achieve success. Engage with your followers by asking if they've ever implemented that strategy and then continuing the conversation by asking about their experience when doing so.

Like yesterday, make the post fun and engaging so that it builds excitement about your future business. Also, be sure to tag me @ericaterryceo on Instagram + use the hashtag #ClassroomtoCEOin30days so that I can show your post some love.

STEP 4 | PRODUCE A SOLUTION-FOCUSED FREEBIE + PRODUCT

DAY 14

F-BOMB! USE WITH CAUTION

As an educator, it's in your nature to give. To achieve success as an educator, you give of yourself tirelessly to ensure that every student achieves learning goals. You'll even miss spending valuable time with your family so that you can get a task done during the evening or on the weekend even though you're technically "off work." You do all of this and never expect to receive one additional penny for your efforts because that's what it takes to be successful and get the job done.

To be successful as an edupreneur, you're going to have to condition your mind to think differently so that you act differently.

Will you work hard as an edupreneur to ensure that every educator who uses your resources can achieve success and reach their goals? Yes, of course, you will!

Will you oftentimes work evenings and weekends as an edupreneur to get the job done? Yes, you most certainly will!

While you'll be doing a lot of the same things as an edupreneur that you already do as an educator, there's one major difference between doing these things with an educator mindset and an edupreneur mindset.

That difference is that when you do these things as an edupreneur, you won't be doing them for free.

One of the big shifts that you must make when transitioning from an educator mindset to an edupreneur mindset is recognizing that time is money.

As an edupreneur, it is important for you to understand that you are worthy and your time is valuable.

Yes, I'm talking to YOU!
Yes, YOU are worth it!
Yes, YOU deserve to get paid for the effort that you put into empowering others.
Yes, YOU!
You deserve to get paid for everything that you do.
Everything?
Well, almost everything.

Let me back up real quick for someone that's going to take what I'm saying to the extreme.

Yes, you deserve to get paid for everything that you do. If you listen to the Classroom to CEO Podcast, you've heard me say it time and time again: "you cannot give away everything for free." In episode 15, I actually refer to the word *free* as an F-Bomb.

Why?

Simply because *Free* is the one word that will kill your chance of achieving edupreneur success when used too often.

But don't get me wrong. Just because I don't believe that you should use the word *free* often doesn't mean that you shouldn't use it at all.

To grow your online business and establish an engaged community, there will be times when you have to unleash that F-Bomb and offer a digital resource for free. That's a fact!

However, when you do so, make sure that you're being strategic and purposeful in your approach. Do NOT unleash that F-Bomb and create a freebie until you have complete clarity about what you're creating and why you're giving it away for free.

Before you decide to give away your resources for free, always, always, ALWAYS create a CEO Success Plan like the one that I described yesterday. This one step will allow you to have complete clarity about how you will eventually earn money from the future products that your freebie leads to.

I don't want to visit your social media page three months from now to find out that you're giving everything away for free. I know it's in your nature to give, give, give, but if you desire to be successful as an edupreneur, you have to learn how to be purposeful in your giving.

You don't just give away something for free for the sake of giving it away for free. No ma'am! No sir! You certainly don't do that.

Instead, when you choose to give away something for free, you do it as a strategic part of your CEO Success Plan.

Let me give you an example of how to use a freebie strategically in my side hustle, Classroom to CEO...

If you go to the Classroom to CEO website (*www.classroomtoceo.com*), you'll discover that I give away the Classroom to CEO Cheat Sheet for free. This cheat sheet provides six simple steps to start and grow an online business, and it provides extreme value because it also includes a plan that someone can use to start their online business without investing any money.

But here's the deal! It provides valuable information that empowers an educator to start a business for free while also allowing them to learn more about my business and the SIMPLE Classroom to CEO revenue system that helped me to create four additional income streams in less than one year. So while I'm giving them a tool that's going to help them take the first steps on their edupreneurial journey, I'm also providing another way for them to get to know me so that we can build a relationship that eventually leads them to engage in my online community. It's a win-win for both of us, and as you'll discover on Day 21, Relationships = Revenue.

See how that works? The customer wins AND you win. You both win when you create a CEO Success Plan that includes a strategic approach to giving away a digital resource for free.

Anytime that you create a CEO Success Plan, it's important for you to not only think about what freebie you're going to give away, but you must also spend time contemplating why you are giving it away.

When deciding whether or not you should invest your time to create a new freebie, consider these questions:

- How will my Favorite Educator benefit from this freebie?
- How will it help her to win?
- How am I going to benefit from this freebie?
- How is it going to help me win by further building and growing my business?

After you consider these questions, if you find that creating a new freebie results in a win-win situation for you and your Favorite Educator, then it's time to move forward with using the FAST Freebie & Product Creation Method to quickly create a Solution-Focused Freebie.

As you've probably guessed, FAST is an acronym that describes four steps that enable you to quickly create a freebie that not only provides lots of value to your Favorite Educator, but also allows them to have a quick win so that they can experience that first taste of success. It's that feeling of success that's going to make them want more, which means that they'll return to actually buy the next product on your CEO Success Plan, which we'll be working together to create this week.

The 4 steps of the FAST Freebie & Product Creation Method are:

Step 1 | Focus on solving just ONE small part of the overall problem

Step 2 | Address the most common complaint related to the problem

Step 3 | Simple solution that educators can easily implement without spending money

Step 4 | Turn the simple solution into a Solution-Focused Freebie & Product that removes barriers and empowers educators to begin overcoming the problem

Just in case you didn't notice, the four steps of the FAST Freebie & Product Creation Method are directly embedded into your CEO Success Plan. This ensures that you stay focused on quickly creating freebies and products that are directly aligned with your CEO Empowerment Statement and that ultimately helps teachers to achieve success.

During today's CEO Success Move, you will plan the Solution-Focused Freebie that you will create tomorrow by implementing the first three steps of the FAST Freebie & Product Creation Method, but before we do that, let's review each of the steps.

Step 1 | Focus on Solving ONE small part of the overall problem

When it comes to creating freebies, it's important to focus on helping educators to solve just one small part of their overall problem. If you help them to solve the entire problem for free, then there's no need for them to purchase anything from you because they are no longer experiencing the problem.

With that being said, your ultimate goal when creating a freebie is to empower your Favorite Educator to experience a quick win so that they have confidence that your step-by-step solution to solve the entire problem actually works. Once they have that confidence, they'll be much more inclined to come back and purchase your next product because they'll want to continue to experience those wins in their life. They know that ultimately your products are helping them to become a better educator and at the end of the day, who doesn't want to get better in their career.

The second step of the FAST Freebie & Product Creation Method goes hand-in-hand with the first step.

Step 2 | Address the most common complaint related to the problem

Let's get real for a moment. Educators complain A LOT. I don't blame them because there's a lot for them to complain about. But here's what you must understand when it comes to your ability to achieve success as an edupreneur.

You can't act upon every complaint that you hear related to your #EducatorProblem. As an edupreneur, it's up to you to cipher through those complaints and identify ONE that's actually within your Favorite Educator's control.

Step 3 | Simple solution that educators can easily implement without spending money

Your goal here is to create a freebie that empowers your Favorite Educator to experience a quick win, which means there can't be any program that requires money attached to it. Your freebie must address the most common complaint by offering a simple, FREE Solution that works!

If the most common complaint can't be solved without having the educator spend money to make it happen, then move to the next complaint because most educators don't control the school or district budget. Most don't have extra money to invest in programs on their own.

Let's look at an example from the work that I do around co-teaching. A common complaint that many co-teachers express is that they struggle to get on the same page when it comes to establishing a collaborative co-teaching relationship. To address this complaint, I offer a freebie that provides co-teachers with a two-week challenge that allows them to take the first steps in developing a stronger co-teaching relationship by showing their co-teacher some love.

Another common #EducatorProblem that I hear from co-teachers is that they don't have common planning time embedded in their schedule to co-plan. Unfortunately, that's outside of the teacher's control. It takes money (i.e., school budget and schedule changes) to solve that issue, so even though it was a common complaint, it was not something that I am able to address with a freebie.

As you can see from this example, my Solution-Focused Freebie wasn't able to solve all co-teaching problems with one quick, fast solution. Despite this fact, I was able to achieve the goal of creating a resource that empowered co-teachers to overcome their #EducatorProblem and achieve a small measure of success. By providing them with electronic resources that enabled them to develop a stronger co-teaching relationship, they were able to begin exchanging ideas and taking a more active role in meeting the needs of all students even while working virtually.

Now it's your turn to plan a Solution-Focused Freebie that empowers educators to achieve a small measure of success.

CEO Success Move #14:

Plan a Solution-Focused Freebie

During today's CEO Success Move, you will implement Steps 1-3 of the FAST Freebie & Product Creation Method to plan a Solution-Focused Freebie.

YOU SHOWED UP.

NOW IT'S TIME TO SHOW OUT!

Today when you Show Out, it will serve a dual purpose. First of all, you'll be announcing to the world that you have an awesome freebie that will be made available soon. Second, you also will be able to validate that your idea really addresses a common complaint that teachers have.

Create a social media post announcing that in the next couple of weeks, you will be sharing a freebie that helps them to _____. Then ask any educators that would like to be the first to try the product to send you a DM or leave a comment with their favorite emoji. Make the post fun and engaging so that it builds excitement, and then tag me @ericaterryceo on Instagram + use the hashtag #ClassroomtoCEOin30days so that I can show your post some love.

DAY 15

PRODUCE A SOLUTION-FOCUSED FREEBIE

Yesterday you implemented Steps 1-3 of the FAST Freebie & Product Creation Method to plan your Solution-Focused Freebie, and later on today, you'll be implementing Step 4 to actually create it. Before you do, we need to talk about a common mistake that I see many edupreneurs make when creating a freebie.

Oftentimes when I work with edupreneurs, I discover that their freebie is a resource that teachers can use with students. It's usually some type of no-prep lesson that may save the teacher some time, but other than that, it does nothing to help them solve their #EducatorProblem.

A large part of the work that I do with co-teachers is helping them transform instructional practices to meet the needs of ALL students. With that in mind, I could easily create a free, digital template that teachers use to help students to scaffold writing assignments. While that may help them save time by not having to create the tool themselves, it doesn't get to the heart of any complaint that I've ever heard a co-teacher make.

Maybe you've heard someone say, "*I can't stand co-teaching because I don't have time to scaffold writing assignments for students,*" but I personally have yet to hear that one, and I work with co-teachers all year long. So had I created a scaffolding freebie, it would have been useful, but it wouldn't have got to the heart of any of the most common complaints that co-teachers struggle with.

Had I chosen to go the route of creating a scaffolding template to offer as a free resource, my business would be just like every other one that provides resources for co-teachers. Even though it would be a useful tool, there wouldn't be anything about that resource that makes my brand stand out in my Favorite Educators' mind enough. Even though she may be thankful to have that resource, it doesn't make a large enough impact in her life that the next time she looks for a co-teaching resource, she goes directly to my website rather than going to Pinterest or a teacher resource marketplace, entering a generic term in the search bar and pulling up hundreds of other resources that were not created by me.

So while it's much easier to create a freebie that includes a simple worksheet that doesn't take a lot of time to create, I promise you that you won't turn any of those freebie-seeking teachers into paying customers using that approach.

On the other hand, when you create a freebie that teachers are not only able to use in the classroom, but that also helps them to solve a specific #EducatorProblem that they're struggling with, I promise that they'll return to buy the next product in your CEO Success Plan.

This was another one of those important lessons that I had to learn the hard way. When I first started my online business, I had no idea what I was doing. I spent months on Google researching how to start an online business. I wasted so much time and money trying to figure it out, and that's exactly what I don't want for you. I don't want you to waste your time and money learning how to create a freebie, or as the guru entrepreneurs like to call it, a lead magnet, the way that I did.

Creating a digital resource can be time-consuming and costly when you don't have the right system in place. The FAST Freebie & Product Creation Method is the exact system that you need to make it happen because it empowers you to create a free, solution-focused resource in a short amount of time without spending a dime of your own money.

For today's CEO Success Move, you are going to create your Solution-Focused Freebie. Before you start, let me remind you that Step 3 of the FAST Freebie & Product Creation Method focuses on implementing a simple solution. Once you've outlined your simple solution, Step 4 requires you to turn that simple solution into a Solution-Focused Freebie that removes barriers and empowers educators to take the first steps in overcoming their #EducatorProblem.

The part of the solution that you introduce in your Solution-Focused Freebie should be one that gets fast results. It shouldn't be hard for your Favorite Educator to accomplish, and she should be able to quickly see results.

If you're using the FAST Freebie & Product Creation Method to create a freebie that can be implemented in the classroom, then not only must you ensure that it aligns with your CEO Empowerment Statement and helps a teacher to solve a small part of their #EducatorProblem, but you must also be sure to include these three important elements:

1. Classroom Freebies must be No-Prep. Teachers already spend enough time planning and prepping for lessons. Creating a freebie that adds to the amount of time they have to spend doing this only adds to their frustration. So no

matter how good your lesson is, if it requires additional prep time, don't make it your freebie.

2. Classroom Freebies must include a way to collect data regarding the students' ability to achieve success as a result of engaging in the lesson. This can easily be accomplished by including some sort of formative assessment at the end of the lesson.

3. Classroom Freebies cannot require the teacher to spend additional money on supplies or programs. Teachers already invest enough of their money in classroom supplies, so the last thing that they need is for you to ask them to spend more money to implement your lesson.

With these three factors in mind, during your Success Move today, you will create a Solution-Focused Freebie that inspires quick action to help your Favorite Educator get immediate results.

CEO Success Move #15:
Create a Solution-Focused Freebie
without spending a dime

During today's CEO Success Move, you will create a Solution-Focused Freebie for FREE!!!

If you haven't already enrolled in the free companion course included with your book purchase, then I highly recommend that you do so right now, because you will have instant access to the step-by-step tutorial video that I created to help you complete Success Move #16.

In this video, I take you behind the scenes as I create a Solution-Focused Freebie and walk you step-by-step through the process that I use so that you can pause the video and implement the same steps as you create your freebie.

No matter if you follow along with me or not when you finish creating your freebie today, don't download it as a pdf and put it out into the world just yet because we'll be adding a few more finishing touches to it later this week.

YOU SHOWED UP.

NOW IT'S TIME TO SHOW OUT!

Today you will continue to build momentum and excitement about the freebie that you just finished creating by sharing a post that describes a few details that you've included in it. As in the previous posts, be sure to make it engaging so that you can interact with your followers who will eventually become your Favorite Educators. Be sure to tag me @ericaterryceo on Instagram + use the hashtag #ClassroomtoCEOin30days so that I can show your post some love.

There are social media templates in the companion course that you can use, or feel free to create your own. Either way, have fun & don't forget to tag me @ericaterryceo on Instagram so that I celebrate your success move because this is a big one!

DAY 16
PLAN YOUR FIRST PRODUCT

Kacey loved the students in her fifth-grade math class. She felt confident that she was impacting their lives in such a way that they'd be able to flourish in middle school and beyond, but each day there was a little voice telling her that there was something more. She believed that she had a bigger role to play, but she wasn't sure what that meant.

Although she wasn't absolutely sure what 'more' consisted of, she began to research and listen to podcasts in hopes that it would help her to figure it out. One day she stumbled across the Classroom to CEO Podcast, and at the very end of the episode, she heard me say...

Hey there, my beautiful educator! Kudos to you for making such an amazing impact on the lives of your students. While there's nothing greater than knowing that you're making a difference in the world, oftentimes it seems like you can still be doing more. Have you ever heard that little voice whispering to you that you were made for more than this? Have you been wondering how you can take your classroom knowledge and use it to inspire others to make a difference in the lives of their students? If so, then it's time for you to begin your

Classroom to CEO journey, and I have exactly what you need to get started. When you go to www.classroomtoceo.com/start, you will be provided with instant access to my edupreneurial startup cheat sheet that equips you with 6 simple steps to start and grow an online business. If you're ready to make the move from the Classroom to CEO, download your FREE cheat sheet at www.classroomto-ceo.com/start today!

As soon as Kacey heard those words, she said, "Yes, I'm ready to begin my Classroom to CEO journey!" She turned off the podcast, went to the website, clicked the Start Now button, and downloaded her free copy of the Classroom to CEO Cheat Sheet.

Instantly she discovered that starting an online business was nowhere near as difficult as she was making it out in her mind to be. She said to herself, "There are only 6 simple steps... I can do this!"

She got to work, and within an hour, she had not only discovered her superpower, but she'd also identified the problem that her online business would help teachers to solve.

Where she was once confused, she now had complete clarity. She was clear on her mission and felt like two tons of bricks had been lifted off her shoulders. Ready to take the next step, she visited the website again and, this time, enrolled in the mini-course, *3 Ways to Start a Side Hustle for Free!* so that she could learn how to create products for her new business.

Kacey's story illustrates the power of using the FAST Freebie & Product Creation Method to develop a Solution-Focused Freebie that empowers your Favorite Educator to achieve a small measure of success and leaves them eager to learn more.

After experiencing the quick win that your Solution-Focused Freebie will provide, your Favorite Educators will revisit your site looking for a way to continue working with you.

When planning and creating the first product in your CEO Success Plan, don't make the mistake of creating a monster size course that includes a robust process that takes weeks or months to achieve the result. Rather than creating one low-cost, rockstar product that blows a teacher's mind and leaves them craving for more of that goodness, many edupreneurs attempt to bundle up a year's worth of lesson plans into one product.

Your first product should not be an attempt to prove that you understand an entire year's worth of curriculum. The purpose of the first product that you will spend time planning and creating over the next few days is very similar to the freebie. You want it to help your Favorite Educator overcome a part of their #EducatorProblem, but not ALL of it.

Remember that you can't solve the entire #EducatorProblem with one product or service!

If you try to do too much or worse, make educators do too much with your first product, they will experience overwhelm, which leads to stress, and that's the opposite of what we're here to do.

You and I, my friend, are called to empower educators to achieve greatness by helping them reduce the stress and overwhelm that they feel in their current role. When we create freebies and products, we focus on solving a small part of the #EducatorProblem so that we don't contribute to the frustration and overwhelm.

The contents of this first product should empower your Favorite Educator to achieve step 2 of your solution, or if your freebie provided the WHAT, the product that you are creating today should provide the HOW.

In Kacey's story, she enrolled in *3 Ways to Start a Side Hustle for Free* so that she could learn HOW to start a side hustle and create her first product.

Just in case you're wondering, my Solution-Focused Product, *3 Ways to Start a Side Hustle for Free*, consisted of video tutorials and a bundle of resources because when I rebranded and launched Classroom to CEO, I already had digital resources that I had created during my early years, which I was able to repurpose to quickly create that mini-course.

If you're just starting out, you won't have resources at your disposal, and I don't recommend that you spend a lot of time creating a bunch of individual resources with the goal of creating a bundle. Trust me, it is not necessary to sell a bundle of resources in order to make your side hustle profitable.

Remember what I told you earlier... KEEP IT SIMPLE!

Create ONE product that allows your Favorite Educator to achieve the next logical step in your solution. If your Solution-Focused Freebie provided the WHAT, then your first Solution-Focused Product can share the details of the HOW.

Another product creation strategy that works well is that if your Solution-Focused Freebie provided step 1 of the solution that you outlined during Success Move #12, then your first product can provide step 2.

This is the strategy that I use when providing educational consulting around the topic of co-teaching. My CEO Empowerment Statement as a consultant is to empower co-teachers to develop strong, collaborative relationships and transform instruction to meet the needs of ALL students, including students with disabilities.

- Solution-Focused Freebie: *Show Your Co-Teacher Some Love Challenge.* This free e-guide provides simple activities that help co-teachers to develop a stronger co-teaching relationship over a two-week period.
- Solution-Focused Product: *Co-Teaching Success Binder.* This toolkit includes digital resources that empower co-teachers to quickly establish roles and responsibilities, organize their classroom procedures, and establish a strong, effective relationship so that they can achieve co-teaching success without stress!

Once again, your ultimate goal is to create ONE product that allows your Favorite Educator to get a taste of what success feels like by achieving the next logical step in your solution.

I cannot reiterate this enough… Keep It Simple!

You are just starting out, and if you try to do too much, too fast, you will sink. I want you to fly towards success, so today, focus on planning ONE Solution-Focused Product. (*Yes, the Power of ONE applies here too!*).

With that being said, are you ready to plan your first Solution-Focused Product?

Of course, you are, so let's do this!

CEO Success Move #16:

Plan a Solution-Focused Product

After creating your Solution-Focused Freebie yesterday, the next logical question to ask yourself is, "What product will my Favorite Educator need to achieve the next step in the solution that I outlined in Success Move #12?"

Depending on the problem that you help educators to solve, this may be a week's worth of lesson plans and activities for the classroom, a fill-in-the-blank workbook, a digital toolkit, or a mini-course, just to name a few. The goal here is to help your Favorite Educator achieve success in step 2 of your solution.

Please note that in a few days, we will get into the specifics of pricing this first product, but it's important to keep in mind that this is a low-cost product. That is why you want to limit it to a small digital resource or mini-course that doesn't require a lot of time and resources for you to create. If you're planning to offer a more robust product such as a six-week course or coaching program, that comes after you've used your freebie and this first product to attract your Favorite Educators and grow your online community.

For today's CEO Success Move, you will plan a low-cost product that your Favorite Educator will use to continue the momentum they gained after using your Solution-Focused Freebie.

YOU SHOWED UP.

NOW IT'S TIME TO SHOW OUT!

Today you are going to begin building momentum and excitement about the product that you just finished outlining by creating a post or story where you tease that it's coming soon. If you create a story, you can quickly show a snapshot of the outline, or if you create a post, you can start counting down to when your new business will be launched (*Guess what? You're more than halfway there. Woo-Hoo!!!! Your online business launch is only 2 weeks away!*)

As in the previous posts, be sure to make it engaging so that you can interact with your followers, who will eventually become your Favorite Educators. Be sure to tag me @ericaterryceo on Instagram + use the hashtag #ClassroomtoCEOin30days so that I can show your post some love.

DAY 17

PRODUCE A SOLUTION-FOCUSED PRODUCT

I could begin this chapter by sharing a story about my first product, but it was such a hot mess that I refuse to even use these precious pages to talk about that catastrophe.

I wish that I could say that I started my online business by creating a rockstar digital resource as my first product using the strategy that I'm sharing with you today, but that's soooo far from the truth.

Ok... Ok... I'll tell you about it. Geez!

Let me start off by saying that the core values of community and empowerment have always been the motivating force behind everything that I do. With that being said, as a frustrated black woman who felt extremely overwhelmed while trying to figure out how to create a profitable online business, my first paid product was... tada... a membership group!

Yes, I skipped all of the other properties and went straight for Boardwalk when I launched the Black Bloggers Network monthly membership group as my first paid product.

Here I was still struggling to figure it all out. I hadn't created any products that helped anyone solve anything. Even worse, I hated blogging. The very act of sitting down every week and writing a blog post made me sick to my stomach. But for some reason, unbeknownst to me, I thought it was a good idea to start a membership group for bloggers.

While I can't tell you why I thought that starting a monthly membership group around a topic that I was still trying to figure out for myself as a newbie was a good idea, what I can tell you is that I got it wrong.

ALL THE WAY WRONG!

As you can imagine, in only a few short months, the Black Bloggers Network went up in flames. I do NOT want your story to be one of an online business gone wrong. While the first product that you create can be a wide array of options, my recommendation, especially if you are brand new and using this book to start your side hustle, is to begin by creating a digital resource, such as an editable template or digital toolkit. Furthermore, if your online business serves teachers that are struggling with instructional practices, then the digital resource that you create should include a no-prep lesson that teachers can easily implement in their classroom and see immediate results.

The advantage of starting your business with a digital resource as your first product is that much like the freebie, digital resources are easy to create, don't take a lot of time, and most importantly, you can create them at a very low cost.

While we won't get into the details of pricing today, just know that your first product should add a whole lot of value to the life of your Favorite Educator without making them spend a lot of money to get it. Your ultimate goal with the first paid product is to allow your Favorite Educator to continue to experience achieving success when using your products, while at the same time getting accustomed to the idea that the value they receive is worth the money that they're spending to continue working with you.

Now that it's almost time for you to create your first product, just like you did with the freebie that you created a couple of days ago, you will use Google Slides or Google Docs to create this digital resource too! 90% of the resources that I create are made using Google Docs or Slides because it costs me $0 to create them.

The key to success when creating a digital resource as your first product is to always remember to keep it SIMPLE! Make sure that it helps educators to solve a specific problem.

Most importantly, don't worry about the graphics or let yourself get intimidated by trying to compete with experienced edupreneurs that have been creating resources for years or, better yet, have a team that creates the resources for them. Don't compare your chapter one to another edupreneurs chapter ten because doing so usually leads to imposter syndrome. As your business grows, you'll be able to get fancier with your images, and one day, you'll be able to afford to add members to your team that do all of the graphic design work for you.

CEO Success Move #17:

Create a Solution-Focused Product

Today's CEO Success Move is very techy, so if the tech scares you, then it's definitely time for you to enroll in the free companion course that's included with your book purchase. On Day 17, you will discover a step-by-step tutorial video that I created to help you complete Success Move #17.

In this video, I take you behind the scenes of my digital products and walk you step-by-step through the process that I use, so that you can pause the video and implement the same steps as you create yours.

No matter if you follow along with me or not, when you finish creating your product today, don't download it as a pdf and start selling it just yet. We'll be adding a few more finishing touches to it over the next couple of days.

YOU SHOWED UP.
NOW IT'S TIME TO SHOW OUT!

Today you will continue to build momentum and excitement about the product that you created by creating a post that shares a few details about it. As in the previous posts, be sure to make it engaging so that you can interact with your followers, who will eventually become your Favorite Educators. Be sure to tag me @ericaterryceo on Instagram + use the hashtag #ClassroomtoCEOin30days so that I can show your post some love.

DAY 18

PRICE YOUR PRODUCT

I'm about to let you in on a little secret...one of the greatest struggles that I had to overcome before I was able to begin experiencing success as an edupreneur was the fact that I had this terrible practice of giving away too much of my time for free.

Like many new edupreneurs, I began my edupreneurial journey while still operating with an educator mindset, which was a huge mistake on my part.

In order to be successful as educators, we get stuck in a routine of bringing work home and working nights and weekends to get everything done. We miss out on precious time with our family because we're planning lessons and grading papers and don't even think anything of it. This routine becomes our norm and happens so often that we tend to overlook it. Much like the Energizer bunny, we keep going and going and going, and as Energizer Educators, we keep doing and doing and doing because that's what it takes for us to make the greatest impact in the lives of our students.

Despite the fact that we're always willing to do whatever it takes to make it happen, at the end of the month, our paycheck is exactly the same. No matter if we work late into the night, arrive at school an hour early and stay an extra hour late, or sit at home grading papers all day on a Sunday, there's no difference in our paycheck.

That cycle of working unlimited hours for no additional pay doesn't work out so well when you're an edupreneur and it most certainly doesn't lead to success. When you give away all that you have without expecting anything in return, you end up getting exactly what you expect… NOTHING!

The harsh reality is that as long as you continue to offer your products and services for free, people will continue to take and use them for free. The bottom line is this —Your Favorite Educators won't pay you for your time and resources until you ask them to. If you don't ask to be paid, you never will get paid. Period.

As a CEO, if your goal is to make your Edupreneur Vision of Success a reality, it's extremely important that you shift from an educator to an edupreneur mindset and realize that your time is valuable. Not only is your time valuable, but you are worthy and deserve to get paid for the hours that you put into creating products that empower other educators to achieve success.

If you don't remember anything else from our 30-day journey together, please remember this: as you continue to put in work to build your online business, as you begin to empower educators to reduce their stress and overcome their problems, as you create amazing resources that equip them to achieve success, always remember that your time is valuable and you deserve to get paid for what you're doing to help others.

Realizing that I had to stop giving away my time for free was only half the battle. Once I made the decision to start charging for my time and resources, I began struggling with another issue — pricing my products.

When it comes to pricing products, I tend to go back and forth in my mind about different prices for days. I'm constantly wondering if the price I'm considering is too high or too low.

But that's not all that my mind thinks about when trying to decide upon a price. This is always the moment that imposter syndrome kicks in. It's when I'm considering what to charge that I begin to have inner thoughts like…

Girl, stop playing! No one will pay you that much for this product.

If you're going to charge that much, you should add more to the product. No one will pay that much if this is all you're going to include.

Sweetie, who do you think you are? They might pay such & such that much for that product, but there's no way that they'll pay you anywhere near that.

Let me tell you that imposter syndrome is a real thing, and no matter how many people you empower through your online business, it NEVER goes away!

I know that pricing products is my imposter syndrome trigger, so when it happens, I come ready to strike back.

See, I'm a God girl. I'm not saying that I'm anywhere near the perfect Christian, but I do trust in God and believe that His word is true. On Day 3 when we talked about developing your success routine, I shared that mine consists of God. Family. Business.

Every morning when I wake up, the first thing that I do is read scriptures and pray. My Edupreneur Success Routine helps me to arm myself with the word of God, and it's these same set of scriptures that I use to strike back when imposter syndrome kicks in.

Imposter Syndrome: *Girl, stop playing! No one will pay you that much for this product.*

I Strike Back with: *"For I know the plans I have for you,"* declares the Lord, *"plans to prosper you and not to harm you, plans to give you hope and a future."* Jeremiah 29:11 NIV

Imposter Syndrome: *If you're going to charge that much, you should add more to the product. No one will pay that much if this is all you're going to include.*

I Strike Back with: *Commit your works to the Lord, and your plans will be established.* Proverbs 16:3 NASB

Imposter Syndrome: *Sweetie, who do you think you are? They might pay such & such that much for that product, but there's no way that they'll pay you anywhere near that.*

I Strike Back with: *"A man's gift makes room for him and brings him before great men."* Proverbs 18:16 NASB

As you continue along this edupreneurial journey, it's not a question of 'if' imposter syndrome will kick in; the question is 'when' imposter syndrome will kick in.

Whenever it appears, be sure that you're ready to strike back, too, because if you don't, it's the seed of doubt that imposter syndrome plants in your mind that will stop you from moving forward in your business.

Your way of striking back against imposter syndrome may look very different from what I described, and that's ok. If scriptures aren't your thing, find quotes or lyrics from your favorite songs. It doesn't matter the source. As long as it empowers you to strike back against imposter syndrome and keep moving forward, then it's the perfect tool for you.

When it comes to pricing, the #1 question that I get asked when helping edupreneurs create their CEO Success Plan is this...

How much should I charge for my first product?

As you've been creating your product, I know that this question has popped in your mind a million and one times, and I promise you that we're going to get there.

Before we talk about the price of your product, I think that it's important that we first talk about the purpose of your product.

When it comes to determining the purpose of a product, many edupreneurs make the mistake of believing that the purpose of every product is always to make a lot of money. Every time they create a new product, they approach it with the mindset of how much money they think they can make from it.

Doing so drives them to keep adding more and more to the product, not because the resources that they're adding will empower their Favorite Educator to overcome their problem at a faster rate, but because they falsely believe that if they add more stuff, then that makes the product more valuable.

What ends up happening is that they have a huge product with many components that look appealing at first sight, but ultimately doesn't achieve the intended outcome of empowering educators to overcome their #EducatorProblem. Their Favorite Educator buys the product, tries it out, and when it doesn't work, they never buy another product again.

If you approach product creation with the mindset of "how much money can I make" rather than "how can I empower my Favorite

Educator to achieve success," then your online business will never reach its full potential.

The purpose of your first product is not to make you rich. It is to introduce your Favorite Educator to your online business and give them a taste of what it feels like to achieve success. When they get that first experience of what success feels like, they will return to your site because they are going to want to experience it again, and next time, they will purchase a more expensive product.

Now that you have a better understanding of the purpose of your product, let's talk about pricing.

Honestly, pricing isn't as hard as most edupreneurs make it out to be. The formula is actually quite simple.

Start low, and with each new product that you release, go higher. It's as simple as that.

Oh, and one more thing. Choose a price that ends in 7. Don't ask me why because I don't have any rhyme or reason except for my best friend Google told me that research has proven that prices that end in the number 7 sell better than those that end in 0, so I'm passing that little nugget on to you.

If you are about to launch your online business for the first time and you're a brand new edupreneur, then let me make this real easy for you. Make sure that your first Solution-Focused Product includes a digital resource that sells for no more than $17. Yep, that's it.

Remember that this is only your starting point. Eventually, you'll create additional products that you'll sell at much higher price points, but with this first product, you're pricing it at $17 (or less.)

If you're an experienced edupreneur that's bundling a lot of resources, then, of course, your price can be higher. But listen here, I don't care how many resources you add to that bundle. It doesn't matter if you've added all of the bells and whistles. Do NOT charge more than

$37. If you're charging $37, then it better be the best product related to your #EducatorProblem on the market. When I say the best, I mean that it should include videos, templates, and printable resources all combined into one AMAZING Product that solves a specific problem.

CEO Success Move #18:

Price Your Product

Pricing digital products is nowhere near as complicated as many edupreneurs make it out to be. Here we make everything SIMPLE, including pricing your products. It really is quite simple.

To complete today's CEO Success Move, choose a price for your product that ends in 7.

YOU SHOWED UP.
NOW IT'S TIME TO SHOW OUT!

Today you will continue to build momentum and excitement about your new business by creating a post about your experience of creating and pricing your first product.

As in the previous posts, be sure to make it engaging so that you can interact with your followers, who will eventually become your Favorite Educators. Be sure to tag me @ericaterryceo on Instagram + use the hashtag #ClassroomtoCEOin30days so that I can show your post some love.

DAY 19

POLISH YOUR PRODUCT

N ow that you've priced your product, it's time to begin thinking about selling it.

On Day 2, I shared with you how I leaned on months of research to start my online business. Whatever the research said, I did.

Well, when it came to selling my first digital product, I made the mistake of once again entrusting in the advice of those gurus that popped up on the first page of my Google search. The terrible advice that they gave was for me to sell the resources from my WordPress website.

To do so required that I invest months into creating a WordPress website and then take even more time trying to figure out how to set up a shop on my WordPress website.

I'll admit that the gurus were right in the fact that selling resources from my own website enabled me to earn more money from each sale because I was only responsible for paying a small fee to PayPal or Stripe versus the large commission that popular teacher resource marketplaces take, but their advice to do it from WordPress was wrong. ALL WRONG!

Please don't repeat the mistake that I made. Rather than wasting months and months trying to figure out how to create a WordPress website to sell your products from, take the simple route that you'll learn about tomorrow.

Before you put it up for sale, it's important for you to add additional info to your freebie and product that keeps your Favorite Educators coming back for more.

So often, edupreneurs make the mistake of believing that their product is only about the content that it includes. If your goal is to make your side hustle profitable, which I know it is because you're more than halfway through our 30-day journey together, then your product has to be about more than just the content.

You should ALWAYS be thinking about how you can bring the educator that's using your product back to engage in your online community. It doesn't matter if they engage with you on social media, through email marketing, or on your website. Your goal is to get them to return to your community and engage, and that's what polishing your product is all about.

When I create digital products, I always create the content first. Once I'm satisfied with the quality of the content and confident that it will help my Favorite Educators to overcome their #EducatorProblem, then I polish it. I do this by adding four finishing touches that increase engagement and lead the customer back to my website to continue engaging within my online community.

- **Finishing Touch #1:** Create a cover page that includes an image + title (or subtitle) that speaks to the #EducatorProblem that's being addressed in the product. Add color to make it stand out and catch the attention of your Favorite Educators.
- **Finishing Touch #2:** On the first page, add a welcome letter. In your welcome, be sure to express your excitement and gratitude that they are using your product and then invite them to join your community. (Don't have a community yet? No worries! I've got you covered. You'll be creating one soon).
- **Finishing Touch #3:** On the last page, create an advertisement for the next product in your CEO Success Plan.
- **Finishing Touch #4:** In the footer, add a sentence that describes the types of resources that they can find on your website (or social media page, if you don't have one yet) and include a direct link to it. For example, in the footer of my resources, you will find a statement such as *"Continue your Classroom to CEO Journey by accessing FREE edupreneur tips and resources at www.classroomtoceo.com."*

CEO Success Move #19:

Polish Your Product

During today's CEO Success Move, you will add additional items to your digital product that makes it more appealing to your Favorite Educator and leads them back to your website to buy the next product in your CEO Success Plan.

If you haven't already enrolled in the free companion course included with your book purchase, then I highly recommend that you enroll right now because when you do, you will have instant access to the step-by-step tutorial video that I created to help you complete Success Move #19.

In this video, I take you behind the scenes and show you exactly how to add each of the finishing touches that you need to polish your digital product.

YOU SHOWED UP.
NOW IT'S TIME TO SHOW OUT!

Today you will continue to build momentum and excitement about your new business by creating a post showing yourself at your laptop putting the finishing touches on your new product.

As in the previous posts, be sure to make it engaging so that you can interact with your followers, who will eventually become your Favorite Educators. Be sure to tag me @ericaterryceo on Instagram + use the hashtag #ClassroomtoCEOin30days so that I can show your post some love.

DAY 20
DON'T STOP! GET IT, GET IT!

"I've been creating and selling resources from Teachers-Pay-Teachers for six months, and I haven't even earned $50!"

Those were the first words that Elaine Parker said to me during our first coaching call. She shared how she had spent the last six months on a mad dash to create as many resources as possible that other high school Physical Science teachers could use in their classrooms.

Like so many other teachers that focus solely on creating and selling resources from popular teacher resource marketplaces, Elaine was operating with the false belief that the more items that she had in her store, the more money she would earn from her business.

I can't begin to tell you the number of edupreneurs that I've met who have shared remnants of this same story in one way or another. Like Elaine, they've poured countless hours into creating and adding new resources to their stores, and at the end of the first year, they've earned less than $100.

What's happening to Elaine and a lot of other educators that sell digital resources from a teacher resource marketplace is that they are putting 100% of their time and effort into building a business where all of their eggs are in one basket. They've heard stories of teachers that have earned enough money to leave the profession and go full time creating and selling digital resources so they pour all of their energy into trying to create that same reality for themselves.

While I won't say that it can't happen, what I will say is that route is a very difficult path that doesn't often lead to edupreneurial success. While no road is easy and all roads to edupreneurial success require lots of hard work and dedication, when you choose a highway that is already very busy, it's very likely that you'll eventually get stuck in a traffic jam. When you get stuck in traffic, you know what happens next. It ends up taking you much longer to reach your final destination, which, in this case, is to EARN MONEY from your side hustle.

Another consequence of taking a busy road is that because it's so saturated, you're very likely to see others that are driving the same make and model car as you. Oftentimes, it's even the same exact color. When this occurs, it is much harder to stand out and get noticed, which, as you'll learn later, is required to achieve success as an edupreneur.

There are many other reasons that I don't recommend putting all of your eggs in the popular online teacher resource marketplace basket, but if you need more convincing, just think about it like this.

I know that it seems very appealing when you go on the Teachers-Pay-Teachers website and read stats like they are the largest teacher resource marketplace for educational resources in the world, with over five million teachers purchasing resources through their platform in 2019.

You read that and immediately begin to think that if 5 MILLION teachers shopped on Teachers-Pay-Teachers in ONE YEAR, then surely you will find at least 100 that will be attracted to your store and buy your products.

Am I right?

Well, the problem is that sooooo many other teachers have created resources that they list there that it's hard to stand out and get noticed on that platform. According to their website, there are currently over 3 million resources, which means that there are thousands of other resources that are similar to what you've created this week.

At this point, starting a TpT store and hoping that you'll be able to create and sell enough resources to make your Edupreneur Vision of Success a reality is much like being a goldfish in a tank with thousands of other goldfish. When placed in the right environment, goldfish have the ability to keep growing until death. Their growth is only limited by environmental factors, such as the size of the bowl and the amount of space that they have to live. So when placed in a tank with thousands of other goldfish, their growth is stunted because there's not enough room for them to continue growing.

I imagine that goldfish has a deep desire to get out of the overcrowded tank that's stunting its growth because it knows that if it could break free, there's an opportunity for it to attain unlimited growth. To get out of the overcrowded tank, it could wait for a little kid that wants a pet to choose it, but that strategy would prove difficult unless it figured out a way to stand out and get noticed. Another option would be for that goldfish to jump into the empty tank that's right next to them.

As an edupreneur, you are faced with the same two choices as the goldfish.

You can choose to build an online business that's solely focused on creating digital resources that you sell from a teacher resource marketplace that is filled with thousands of other teachers that are creating and selling resources that look just like yours, or you can choose to jump into the empty tank that provides you with the opportunity to experience unlimited earning potential by creating multiple streams of income.

That's exactly what I'm offering you when you implement the SIMPLE 6 Step Classroom to CEO System that I teach in this book.

When you decide to jump into the less crowded tank and focus on building an online business that includes multiple streams of income, you will experience freedom and flexibility that extends far beyond what you could ever achieve as a teacher seller.

You will be able to work in your pj's, stop to pee whenever you feel like it, cook breakfast for your kids, and be the parent in the carpool lane before and after school.

You will have the energy to help with homework while you cook dinner.

When you put the kids to sleep, you can actually turn on the TV and enjoy your favorite show while it's on rather than always having to wait until the weekend to watch it on demand.

You won't have to worry about bills or dream of vacations that you'll never be able to afford because you'll be on that Disney cruise before you know it if that's what your heart desires.

Most importantly, you'll spend your days doing what you love and empowering other educators to achieve success.

The first 30 days of your journey to edupreneurial success will begin with creating and selling digital resources, but it won't end there. The key to your success as an edupreneur lies in the fact that you are focused on creating not just one additional stream of income, but

MULTIPLE streams of income. In my best Luke voice, I'm telling you, "Don't Stop! Get It, Get It!"

The online business that you will establish in our 30-day journey will help you to create your FIRST income stream, but as you continue to engage in this community, you will learn how to grow your business by continuously creating additional streams of revenue, one new product at a time.

See, there's one huge difference between a teacher seller and a CEO. Teacher sellers focus on creating a large variety of different digital resources that they sell from their store. As a CEO, your focus is on creating multiple streams of income. Even though you may start by selling digital resources, you won't stay there. You will continue to expand your business with new products and services until one day you look up and you've built an empire.

Remember our Classroom to CEO manifesto:

We are Purpose Driven Edupreneurs that
Create multiple streams of income
Empower others to achieve success
Operate with a successful edupreneur mindset

During today's CEO Success Move, you will create your FIRST income stream, but trust and believe me when I tell you that it won't be your last. Using the step-by-step video tutorial included in the companion course, you will set up and sell your product from your own FREE website that doesn't require a lot of time or tech skills to create.

This success move will allow you to create a new income stream, but here's what you should know. The additional income stream that you will begin to create today simply lays the foundation and allows you to experience earning a little extra income. Selling digital resources alone will NOT allow you to make your Edupreneur Vision of

Success a reality. But I know you. You are purpose-driven and committed to showing up and doing the work. As you continue to do the work, grow your audience, and add revenue streams to your online business, you will look up one day and discover that you've built an empire.

CEO Success Move #20:

Build Your Own Site to Sell Products

Today, your CEO Success Move is to create your own place in the online world. Check out Day 20 in the companion course for a step-by-step video tutorial that shows you how to purchase the URL for your Drop the MIC Name and create a site for less than what you would spend on a meal from your favorite restaurant.

Don't believe me?

Login to the companion course right now to achieve success by quickly creating a site to sell your resources!

YOU SHOWED UP.

NOW IT'S TIME TO SHOW OUT!

Take a screenshot of your new site & share it on social media to let your friends, family, and teacher friends know that it's coming soon. Tag me @ericaterryceo on Instagram + use the hashtag #ClassroomtoCEOin30days so that I can show your post some love.

STEP 5 | LIST BUILD LIKE PROS

DAY 21
RELATIONSHIPS = REVENUE

The Tale of Two Edupreneurs

Meet Lucy Walker. Lucy can best be described as a go-getter! As a teacher, everyone always complimented her willingness to go above and beyond. Anytime there was a new committee or program, Lucy was always invited to be a part of the team because everyone knew that she would do whatever it takes to get the job done.

When Lucy began her edupreneurial journey, she dove in feet first and made it her goal to turn all of her best lesson plans into digital resources in 100 days. Every day she taught all day, then stayed up half the night creating new resources. In addition to creating resources, her weekends were spent creating pins and social media posts while engaging in Facebook groups to also share posts with other teacher sellers.

Lucy did this day in and day out for 100 days. With all of her effort, she was also able to make a few sales, but after she paid upwards of 40% in commission fees, the end result was she earned $27.33. Lucy figured that $27 was better than nothing, but she felt frustrated because she'd worked really hard, so $27 didn't feel like it was enough. Her earnings certainly did not match her effort.

Meet James Bell. James wasn't the most organized teacher under the sun. Honestly, his classroom looked like a tornado had hit it. Old classwork and textbooks were scattered everywhere. Unlike Lucy, who was invited to take part in everything, James was never invited to join a new committee because most of his colleagues didn't think that he was all that dependable. Despite his colleagues' disdain for him, ask any student who their Favorite Teacher was, and 90% of the time Mr. Bell's name made the list. Students and parents alike loved him because, although he was an unorganized mess, he was great at building relationships. He listened and got to know his students in a way that made them feel like they belonged in his classroom. He always made sure to keep parents in the loop and was a technology wizard that used electronic student portfolios to consistently document their progress towards meeting the learning targets.

When James began his edupreneurial journey, he understood that using technology in the classroom and building relationships with students and families were his strengths. When developing his CEO Empowerment Statement, he combined his love for both technology and relationship building. He decided to start an online business that empowered other teachers to use technology to create strong relationships with students and families. In his first 100 days, he used his CEO Success Plan to develop one Solution-Focused Freebie and two Solution-Focused Products that were aligned to his CEO Empowerment Statement.

James's CEO Success Plan was updated after he completed his first 30-day Classroom to CEO journey to include the following:

- Solution-Focused Freebie: A digital resource that explained how student portfolios and automated newsletters can be used to help build strong, collaborative relationships with parents.
- Solution-Focused Product #1: A $7 digital resource and step-by-step video tutorial that provided teachers with the tools that they need to create student portfolios and automated newsletters that help them to build strong, collaborative relationships with parents.
- Solution-Focused Product #2: A $97 online course that equipped teachers with easy-to-implement strategies to further engage parents beyond the newsletter and empower them to take an active role in the development of their students' portfolios.

Within his first 100 days, James earned thousands of dollars and built a community of over 500 of his Favorite Educators. Unlike Lucy, he was thrilled with his results. He felt that his earnings matched his effort, and he knew that he was on the right path to achieve edupreneurial success.

When it comes to edupreneurial success, there's one factor that made James achieve success at a higher level than Lucy. Obviously, it wasn't the amount of work that led to success because Lucy was working hard day and night for 100 days straight.

The one factor that allowed James to create a successful online business was that he focused on empowering his online community to achieve success. While you may be thinking that nurturing a strong community isn't really that important, there is nothing further from the truth.

A common misconception among edupreneurs is that if you create a ton of resources, then educators will buy them. If no one is buying their resources, they convince themselves that it's because they don't have enough in their store yet, and they continue to create more and more digital resources until they burn out. Many edupreneurs approach their business with the belief that if they have a store full of resources, then they'll earn a lot of money, but unfortunately, nothing is further from the truth.

Here's the deal... If you can't attract customers to purchase the first few products that you sell, then guess what?

Even if you have one hundred products, but still don't have any customers, then you ain't gon' earn no money.

For those of you that didn't quite understand my country grammar, let me say it in a way that you understand.

A store with no customers doesn't earn any money no matter how many resources you have in it!

That's why it's extremely important as an edupreneur to grow an online community where you provide value and nurture relationships.

Relationships = Revenue, and don't you forget it!

If you establish an online business that consists of a loyal community of educators that are inspired and empowered by the content in your freebie, they will come back to buy your first product. When that works, they'll come back to buy the next product, and the cycle will continue.

At this point, I hear you saying, "Erica, how can I possibly nurture strong relationships within my online community?" I promise you that tomorrow we're going to get to the how.

But before we discuss the details of how to nurture a community, we must gain clarity about who we should target to be a part of it.

Yes, your community should be filled with your Favorite Educators, but when it comes to building your online community, you want to toss out a wide net. This is the only place where I recommend you be very broad and try to reach everyone. If your Favorite Educator is an Algebra teacher, don't just build a community for Algebra teachers. Build one for middle and high school math teachers so that if they don't teach Algebra right now, but due to a schedule change, they end up teaching Algebra next year, they'll already be in your community and look to you as the expert in all things Algebra.

Got it?

Awesome! So let's identify who is going to be in your community.

CEO Success Move #21:

Establish an Online Community

Your CEO Success Move for today is to identify exactly who to target to be a part of your online community. I provide additional tips on choosing the right community members inside of Day 21 of the companion course.

YOU SHOWED UP.
NOW IT'S TIME TO SHOW OUT!

Today you will continue to build momentum and excitement about your new business by creating a *Coming Soon* post that shares information about your new community. This information can include items such as a list of who's right for your community or a post where you ask your Favorite Educators to leave a comment, tag a friend, or send you a DM.

As in the previous posts, be sure to make it engaging so that you can interact with your followers, who will eventually become your Favorite Educators. Be sure to tag me @ericaterryceo on Instagram + use the hashtag #ClassroomtoCEOin30days so that I can show your post some love.

DAY 22
THE KEY TO BUILDING STRONG RELATIONSHIPS

J ust in case you missed it yesterday, let me say it again.

Relationships = Revenue

Got it?

One more time for the people in the back.

Relationships = Revenue.

It sounds like a simple concept, but in reality, it can be very complicated. Just like in life, establishing real relationships in business takes time to nurture. The biggest issue when it comes to nurturing relationships with your Favorite Educators lies in the fact that as an edupreneur, your time is very limited.

That's right, time or lack thereof is one of the biggest struggles that you'll encounter as an edupreneur, especially if this business is a side hustle!

Just like your experience in your current role as an educator, feeling like you're always pressed for time, the same will be true in your business.

Trust me. Time is a precious commodity, especially for new edupreneurs.

As a new edupreneur, you will find yourself always busy while you figure out how to implement automated systems that help you become more efficient in running your business.

You'll be busy creating resources and learning the essentials of graphic design.

You'll be busy writing emails and engaging on social media with your followers.

I cannot stress to you enough that the word 'busy' will be the biggest understatement when it comes to your life as a new edupreneur.

But here's the deal. Successful edupreneurs understand that they must dedicate time each week to nurture strong relationships within their community. You're here because you want to start a side hustle and achieve success in building your online business, right? Of course, you do! That's why today we're going to talk about how to build a strong community.

While there are many ways that edupreneurs can nurture relationships, the one that I highly recommend for new edupreneurs is to communicate using an automated email marketing system.

Building your email list and using email marketing strategies to develop strong relationships with your Favorite Educators is one of the most important steps you can take to grow your online business. The best part is that once you have the automated system in place that we're going to create over the next four days, it doesn't take a whole lot of time to nurture relationships with your community.

There are many benefits to having an email list, but the main one is that it allows you to showcase your expertise by continually sharing tips that empower your Favorite Educators to achieve success. When you share tips, tools, and resources every week that help them to grow, they are primed and ready to try out the new products that you create.

Building your email list is so important to your success as an edupreneur that we will be working together to List Build Like PROS for the next four days. Before you even ask, yes, PROS is an acronym that provides an overview of the 4 steps that you must take to create an engaged community using email marketing.

List Build Like PROS

Step 1| **Provider**
Step 2| **Really** good gift
Step 3| **O**pt-in landing page
Step 4| **Say** something

Today our focus is on Step 1| **Provider**.

The simplest way to communicate regularly with your community is by using an email provider that automates your email sequences so that once you've set it up, there's nothing left for you to do besides attract new subscribers.

Finding an email provider that allows you to set up automated email sequences is vitally important to your overall success as an edupreneur because your time will be limited. The last thing that you have time to do is to spend hours each week using your Gmail account to draft individual emails to your active community members. Trust me when I tell you that as your business grows, which it will when you implement the SIMPLE Classroom to CEO system, you won't have time to create individual emails to hundreds of community members.

Instead, when you use an automated email provider, you can draft the email one time, and with one click of a button, it goes out to everyone on your email list, including new people that join at a later date. Yes, the Power of ONE is relevant here too!

Another advantage of using an automated email provider is that you can create beautiful landing pages that allow you to automatically collect email addresses and send out emails without having to do any additional work. The best part is that you can do this even if you don't have your own website!

In a couple of days from now, I'll be showing you exactly how to create a professional landing page to collect email addresses. Don't worry if you're not tech-savvy because there will be a step-by-step video tutorial included in the companion course. Also, don't worry if you don't have your own website, because you don't need one. When you choose the right provider, which is exactly what you're going to do during today's CEO Success Move, you will be able to make it happen!

CEO Success Move #22:

Choose the Right Provider

Your CEO Success Move for today is to choose the right provider and set up the basic information that you need to implement an automated email system. Included in Day 22 of the companion course is a list of my favorite automated email providers, as well as a step-by-step video tutorial that shows you how to make today's success move.

YOU SHOWED UP.
NOW IT'S TIME TO SHOW OUT!

Today you will let me know that you made Success Move #22 by commenting on the Instagram post linked in the companion course that shares the name of the automated email provider that you chose. Check out the comments in that post to find out which automated email providers other edupreneurs are choosing as well. See you tomorrow!

DAY 23
AN UNFORGETTABLE FIRST DATE

When I was fifteen years old. I was outside dancing to MC Hammer's *Can't Touch This* with a group of friends. I was snapping my fingers, moving my hips, and shaking my head back and forth to the music until I got a bit too carried away with my dance moves and lost track of what was around me.

BOOM!

I hit my head on the corner of a porch that was completely made up of large rocks. The blow didn't knock me out, but it hurt like hell.

Up until that day, I had perfect, 20/20 vision, but the blow caused my vision to begin gradually deteriorating, and a year later, I began wearing glasses.

The fact that my vision is steadily declining and I have a history of glaucoma in my family makes it extremely important that I get a yearly eye exam. Back in the day, the only option to test for eye disease was to have drops added to dilate the eyes, which meant that you wouldn't be able to see clearly and drive your vehicle for a couple of hours. Knowing that, I'd always schedule my yearly eye exam at the mall so that I could spend that time indulging in one of my favorite activities — shopping!

One year in my early 20s, I decided that I didn't want to spend my time shopping alone. Right before my appointment began, I called a guy that I'd been talking to on the phone but had never gone out on a date with and asked him to meet me at the mall. Yes, I was a 'fast little thang' as my grandma would lovingly call me. LOL!

By the time my eye exam was over and my new glasses were picked out, I walked out of the vision store to find him sitting on a bench with a gift in hand.

It was our first time spending time together, and his first action was to give me a gift. I was immediately smitten. For the next two hours, as we went in and out of stores, I felt like I was walking on air. It's been 20 years since that day, and I still remember how special I felt during those two hours. It was definitely what I would call an unforgettable first date.

Starting that first date off with a gift and then continuing to woo me for the next two hours definitely made him stand out in my mind. Not only that, but the relationship continued to blossom, and we went on more and more dates after that.

While you may not be dating your Favorite Educators in the physical sense, every time someone new begins to interact with your online business, it is very much like you're taking them on the first date. You want to be memorable and stand out in their mind so that they'll come back and continue to build a relationship with you. One of the best ways to do this is by giving them a really good gift upon first meeting them.

When you start the relationship by giving your Favorite Educators a really good gift, it makes them feel valued, even if they don't know you that well. That's why the second step in the List Build Like PROS Strategy is to give a **Really** good gift.

Not only does offering a really good gift help you to make a great first impression, but the truth of the matter is that we serve teachers, and teachers love to get free stuff. Your Favorite Educator will be much more likely to subscribe to your email list and give up her email address if you give her a really good gift in return.

If you're racking your brain trying to figure out what you can give away as your Really good gift, stop right now because I have some exciting news to share with you.

Are you ready for it?
Are you sure?
Ok, here you go...

The Solution-Focused Freebie you created during Success Move #15 will serve as the Really Good Gift that you're going to give away!

Yay!!!!

Are you as excited as I am that you don't have to spend any more time creating another resource? I know that I am.

While you don't have to create an entirely new resource, there are a few steps that you must take to convert it from a Solution-Focused Freebie to a Really Good Gift. The good news is that you don't have to figure it out on your own. I walk you through each of these steps in today's success move.

Are you ready to turn your Solution-Focused Freebie into a Really Good Gift?

Awesome! Let's do it!

CEO Success Move #23:
Turn your Solution-Focused Freebie into a Really Good Gift

Your CEO Success Move for today is to turn the freebie that you've created and polished into a really good gift.

During Success Move #19, you polished your freebie by adding a few finishing touches. Today you're going to use the step-by-step video tutorial included in Day 23 of the companion course to add a few more tweaks to those finishing touches to make sure that your freebie is the really good gift that makes it an unforgettable first date.

YOU SHOWED UP.
NOW IT'S TIME TO SHOW OUT!

Today you will continue to build momentum and excitement about your new business by creating a post highlighting the fact that you just added the finishing touches to your new freebie.

As in the previous posts, be sure to make it engaging so that you can interact with your followers, who will eventually become your Favorite Educators. Be sure to tag me @ericaterryceo on Instagram + use the hashtag #ClassroomtoCEOin30days so that I can show your post some love.

DAY 24

HOW TO MAKE A FIRST IMPRESSION THAT LEADS TO A "YES"

Imagine this...a few months ago, you were on an unforgettable first date, but unfortunately, that relationship didn't work out. After watching you mope around the house for the last few weeks, your best friend convinces you to go on a speed date TONIGHT. With only a few minutes to spare, you throw on your best outfit and rush out the front door.

You've just spent the last few rotations talking to the most boring people. The bell rings, you switch seats, and out of nowhere, your dream spouse is sitting in front of you.

You have one minute to convince this person that you're the cream of the crop and that no one else in the room even comes close to what you have to offer.

So what do you say?

A: You start by spitting out your resume (i.e., education level and career track) and then end with a snapshot of your future life plans.

B: You skip the resume spill and instead start the conversation off with compliments and by speaking encouraging words that build the other person up, and then you share the value that you'd bring and end with an invitation to explore the possibilities further.

Which option, A or B, do you think would make the person that you've been dreaming of your entire life that's now magically sitting across from you say "yes"?

I can't speak for you, but it would be an easy "yes" for me if someone began the conversation with compliments and by uplifting me with words of encouragement, then shared details about how the relationship would benefit me. As soon as they extended the invitation to pursue the relationship further, I'd quickly reply with, "Yes, sir. Where do I sign up?"

While you won't be physically dating the members of your online community, I want you to think of list-building like a first date because it is the first time that your Favorite Educator will actually meet and engage with you.

The third step to List Build Like PROS is the **O**pt-in page.

Just like the speed dating scene above, your Opt-in page is your opportunity to make a first impression that lasts. This may be the only opportunity to convince someone to accept the Really Good Gift that you're offering in exchange for their email address, which is the key factor that makes list building and email marketing so critical to your success as an edupreneur.

When you randomly add a freebie to your online store that anyone can download at any time without having to give you anything in exchange to receive it, a teacher can, in essence, download it, sit across from you on a speed date, and then decide to move to the next table and never interact with your online business again.

By getting an email address before the teacher ever sits down at the table and begins to engage in the speed date, you can keep the conversation going past that first dating experience, no matter how terrible it may have gone.

Think of your Opt-in page as the speed date. It's your opportunity to make a first impression that leads your Favorite Educator to say "yes." Just like with a real speed date, you only have a minute to say everything you need to make it happen. As the saying goes, "you never have a second chance to make a first impression," and that's completely true when it comes to your Opt-in page.

With the click of a button, a person can hit the "x" and be gone forever. That's exactly what we don't want to happen, so today, I'm going to share the five steps you can take during your CEO Success Move to make a FIRST impression that results in a "yes."

At this point, it's clear that I'm obsessed with acronyms, so of course, "FIRST" is capitalized because it represents an acronym for the elements that must be included in your opt-in page for you to make a great FIRST impression.

To create an opt-in page that makes a great FIRST impression, it must include the following five elements:

1. **F**eel good headline: Create a headline that speaks to the problem and/or solution that you're providing.
2. **I**nvite them to opt-in: Make a very specific request (also referred to as a Call To Action) that tells the person exactly what you're asking them to do (i.e., Sign Up Now).
3. **R**eveal benefits: State exactly what they will receive and the benefits they will enjoy as a result of accepting your free gift in exchange for their email address.
4. **S**ay thank you: After they give you their email address, redirect them to a page where you thank them and welcome them to your community.

5. **Treat them to more gifts:** The only thing better than one really good gift is a lot of really good gifts. During tomorrow's CEO Success Move, I will teach you specifically how to turn this one good gift into many.

Now that you know the elements that you must include to make a great FIRST impression, it's time to make your opt-in page.

CEO Success Move #24:

Create an Opt-In Page that Makes a FIRST Impression
that Leads Your Favorite Educator to Say "Yes"

As you create your Opt-in page during today's CEO Success Move, imagine yourself sitting across from your Favorite Educator. Your goal is to create a landing page that grabs their attention and leads them to say "yes" to giving you their email address.

Included in Day 24 of the companion course is a step-by-step video tutorial that helps you design a landing page that will ensure that you make a great FIRST impression.

YOU SHOWED UP.

NOW IT'S TIME TO SHOW OUT!

You are soooo close to being able to start inviting people to join your community, so keep creating posts to build momentum and excitement about your new business. Today you can create a story or short video post showing your opt-in landing page to let people know that it's coming soon.

As in the previous posts, be sure to make it engaging so that you can interact with your followers, who will eventually become your Favorite Educators. Be sure to tag me @ericaterryceo on Instagram + use the hashtag #ClassroomtoCEOin30days so that I can show your post some love.

DAY 25
THE REAL SILENT KILLER

Congratulations! Not only did you make a CEO Success Move during your speed date yesterday, but dang on it! You were also able to walk out of that speed date with your Favorite Educators email address. I'm so proud of you!

Much like when you're hanging out with your friends, and they witness you exchange numbers with someone you just met, the first question is always, "What are you going to do? Are you going to call?"

Well, I have that same question.

You got those digits, oops...email address. So what are you going to do with it now?

A: Over the next two weeks, send out the automated welcome email sequence that you'll create during today's CEO Success Move, and then communicate only when you have a new product to share.

B: Over the next two weeks, send out the automated welcome email sequence that you'll create during today's CEO Success Move, and then continue to communicate weekly to provide tips, resources, and the occasional product announcement.

While I don't want to rain on your parade, I have to be honest and tell you that getting an email address is much like getting a phone number. If you never use it, you won't ever move past the initial meeting phase of your relationship. So if you choose option A, you won't get very far in the quest to develop strong relationships within your online community.

Someone passing gas silently and stinking up an entire room is oftentimes referred to as a silent killer. When it comes to edupreneurship, not using the email address to send messages regularly is the real silent killer for your online business.

Nothing kills your online business more than silence. When people don't hear from you regularly or if they only hear from you when you're trying to sell them something, then their trust dwindles, and eventually, they'll leave the community by hitting that unsubscribe button. This is why it is vitally important for you to say something after the First Date and every week after.

Therefore by choosing option B and communicating weekly through email, you have a much better chance of turning the educator that initially came to your opt-in page for the free gift into a paying customer.

Like with any great relationship, consistency and a clear communication channel are the keys to success. I recommend that consistent, clear communication channels be in the form of a weekly newsletter or email. Teachers create and send newsletters to their students' families all the time, which is why they understand the value that newsletters can hold.

Sending a weekly email sounds simple, right?

I thought so, too... initially.

Shortly after I started my online business and first began to gain new subscribers, I was excited about the opportunities that were ahead.

I would sit at my computer to draft an email, and rather than writing the inspirational words that I was hoping, I would sit there stuck... for hours... trying to figure out what to say.

It eventually got to the point where I could never figure out the right words, so I simply stopped trying to. Rather than providing tips that motivated my community to take action, I was quiet for months and didn't send an email until I was ready to launch a new product.

I'm sure you can guess what happened next.

I launched my new product and sent a series of emails to announce it. The open rate on that email series was below 10%, and those that actually opened the emails rarely clicked the link to learn more about my product.

The result was that I launched to crickets and ended up with almost no sales.

This experience taught me that silence is the greatest killer to your ability to make your Edupreneur Vision of Success into a reality.

Building trust should be the primary purpose of your weekly email.

Staying in constant communication with the Favorite Educators on your email list allows them to get to know you on a more personal level. They get to know your voice, and when the tips that you provide every week help them begin to overcome their problems and let them know that they're not alone, they begin to trust you.

CEO Success Move #25:

Create a template for your weekly email

If you chose an automated email provider during Success Move #22, then it is very likely that they have a variety of templates that you can choose from to craft and send a weekly email. Decide what important information you want to include in your weekly email, and then create a template that you can easily update every week.

Be sure to check out the step-by-step tutorial video that I included on Day 25 of the companion course. In it, I take you behind the scenes and show you exactly how I develop the weekly email that I send out to the Classroom to CEO Crew.

YOU SHOWED UP.

NOW IT'S TIME TO SHOW OUT!

Today you will create a post that shares the types of tips and resources that you are planning to share in your weekly newsletter, and you will invite your Favorite Educators to join your community.

As in the previous posts, be sure to make it engaging so that you can interact with your followers, who will eventually become your Favorite Educators. Be sure to tag me @ericaterryceo on Instagram + use the hashtag #ClassroomtoCEOin30days so that I can show your post some love.

STEP 6 | ENGAGE AS AN EXPERT

DAY 26

WHAT'S YOUR SUPERHERO NAME?

Storm

Flash

Falcon

Incredible Hulk

What do all of these names have in common? Yes, they're names of superheroes, but dig a little deeper and think back to the lesson that you learned on Day 10.

Before you made your CEO Success Move and crafted Your Drop the MIC Name, we discussed the importance of having a memorable name that clearly communicates your mission without you having to say another word.

This same principle applies when it comes to sharing how you help educators to achieve the success that you described when you crafted your CEO Empowerment Statement in Success Move #9.

At this point, you've successfully created a product that will help you to unleash your superpower and do some good in the world of education. But before you get out there and begin saving educators all over the world by helping them to overcome their problems, we have to make sure that you have the right Superhero name.

Let's go back to the superheroes that I named earlier, Storm, Flash, Falcon, and Incredible Hulk. Compare and contrast their names with other superheroes like Jean Grey, Professor X, Captain America, and Thor. Have you figured out the main difference that distinguishes group A from group B?

Group B, which includes Jean Grey, Professor X, Captain America, and Thor, all have names that give no indication of the magnitude or impact of their superpower. On the other hand, Group A, which includes Storm, Falcon, Flash, and Incredible Hulk have names that provide at least a little insight into their powers even if you've never met them and don't know anything about them.

If I did a Google search for someone to quickly help me pick up a package from the other side of town and I was scrolling through a list of names, which one would make me stop scrolling and click the link that takes me to their website? Jean Grey or Flash?

If I was searching for someone to help me train my bird, would I stop to click on Thor or Falcon?

That's how you must think when it comes to giving yourself an expert title. Think of your title as your superhero name. When choosing it, consider what will make your Favorite Educator stop scrolling to click onto your site.

As an educator, you have been blessed with superpowers that you've so graciously used to make a positive impact on the lives of your students. Now it's time to take your level of impact to the next level and use your unique gifts and talents to empower other educators all across the globe.

My expert title, Edupreneur Success Coach, doesn't provide any information as to HOW I will help an edupreneur achieve success. It doesn't go into any details regarding the specific strategies that I use, but it immediately communicates WHAT the end result will be. It's simple, clear, and communicates the outcome.

Your CEO Success Move today will be to craft an expert title that clearly communicates your superpower. Keep in mind that your expert title is not the end-all, be-all. Superhero names such as Storm, Flash, Falcon, and the Incredible Hulk don't tell us everything about the complexities of their superpowers, but it gives us enough information to pique our curiosity. That's exactly what you want your title to do for you. You want it to pique someone's curiosity enough to continue the conversation and learn more about how you can help them to overcome their problems.

CEO Success Move #26:
Craft a Clear, Concise Superhero Name
(i.e., Expert Title)

During today's CEO Success Move, you will craft a clear and concise expert title that communicates your superpower to your Favorite Educator.

> # YOU SHOWED UP.
> ## NOW IT'S TIME TO SHOW OUT!

Congratulations on crafting your Expert Title! I am so very proud of you for showing up and doing the work!

Now that you have an expert title, it's time to share it with the world. Create a social media post that shares your expert title and tag me @ericaterryceo on Instagram + use the hashtag #ClassroomtoCEOin30days so that I can show your post some love.

DAY 27

CHOOSE ONE SOCIAL MEDIA PLATFORM & ENGAGE

On Day 9, I shared with you all my secret obsession with the cartoon version of *X-Men*, but that was only the beginning of my love for superhero TV series. There was *Arrow*, *Heroes*, and *Smallville*, just to name a few of the shows that I've binged on over the years. The whole idea of having supernatural powers has always fascinated me.

Just in case you've never heard of or watched *Smallville*, it was a show based upon the life of Clark Kent, aka Superman. What has always fascinated me about Superman is that in his real life, Clark Kent was just an ordinary joe. There was nothing about him that made him stand out enough for the people that he interacted with on a daily basis to ever believe that he was Superman.

This everyday, ordinary joe persona is the same one that I see in most educators. I'd be willing to guess that your students, other educators in your building, and maybe even your family members don't recognize the superpower that lies within you. When people look at you, they don't envision you as someone that will launch an online business that's going to empower educators all over the world to achieve success.

They may not see the superpower that lies within you, but I do. You have made it to Day 27, which tells me that you've been showing up, doing the work, and showing out every day, so trust and believe when I tell you that, I see you.

I see the vision that you have.

I see the work that you've put in.

I see the fear that continuously tries to creep in and tell you that your dream will never happen.

I see you continuing to move forward despite those fears.

I see you, and I want you to know that your time is near.

Everything that you've always dreamed of is right there waiting on you to act.

But here's the deal… for you to achieve success as an edupreneur, you must be willing to throw on your superhero cape and put yourself out there, which is a lot easier said than done. I talked about it before, but I have to bring it up again because Imposter Syndrome is real.

The first time that you put on your cape and prepare to fly into your purpose, a sense of fear will likely enter your heart that makes you say to yourself, "No one will take my advice. Who'd actually believe that I'm an expert?"

I promise you that it's going to happen. When it does, be prepared to use those scriptures and quotes that you compiled during CEO Success Move #3 to strike back, and most importantly, do it anyways! Keep flying forward into your destiny no matter how you feel!

There's no better place to fly and get connected to other educators across the world than social media. As in all things, even as we engage as an expert, we do so following the principle of the Power of One. This principle applies even when we put on our cape and go out into the world. When you begin to engage with educators as the expert you are, it is very important that at the beginning of your edupreneurial journey, you limit yourself to engaging on only one social media platform.

Start with ONE. As your business grows, you can then begin to add virtual assistants to your team that can help you expand. For example, if you start building your social media platform on Instagram, after you gain an audience there and start earning money from your online business, you then hire someone to create a post. When you've hired a virtual assistant, that's when you begin building your Facebook, Twitter, TikTok, and Pinterest accounts. If you try to do it all yourself right now at the beginning of your journey, you will get overwhelmed and end up burning out.

To ensure that your social media strategy doesn't leave you feeling stressed out and overwhelmed, your CEO Success Move today will be two-fold. First, you will choose ONE social media platform to engage with, and then you will create a 7-day social media strategy that you will wash, rinse, and repeat weekly.

CEO Success Move #27:

Unleash the Power of ONE Social Media Platform

Choose ONE social media platform to engage as an expert and plan a 7-day social media strategy.

When it comes to choosing ONE social media platform, the formula is simple. Choose your favorite and go! Don't worry about how many educators are on there or what other edupreneurs are doing. Start wherever you feel most comfortable because remember, this is only the beginning. You will grow your side hustle to a point that you'll be able to expand to new platforms in the future.

Step 1 | Choose ONE social media platform to engage on as an expert

I am nowhere near anyone's social media guru. Truth be told, if there was one thing that I could totally live without, it would be creating posts and thinking of captions for my social media feed. I love connecting on social media, but it's hard for me to create posts and stories. I tend to worry about how the post looks and wonder if my words will be inspirational enough to drive someone to take action so much so that I've implemented a social media strategy that allows me to attract new customers in as little as 2 hours/week. Wondering how? Join me in the book study group where I provide you with a behind-the-scenes look at ALL of the steps of the Classroom to CEO social media strategy!

I'm saying all of this to say that I don't have a magic formula that will get you thousands of new followers in the next few weeks. As a matter of fact, I don't even believe in focusing on followers AT ALL. Your focus should be to inspire, empower, and provide extreme value no matter how many followers you have. I don't care if it's one hundred or one million people following you, inspire, empower, and provide extreme value every day.

When it comes to your social media strategy, the only 'rule' that I suggest you follow is to post at least ONE time a day on the ONE platform that you choose.

ONE platform, ONE time a day.

Of course, you can always do more, but remember to keep it SIMPLE! Create a schedule that you will be able to maintain without stressing yourself out to do it. Keep it SIMPLE, and don't get caught up in the "You have to post this many times per day" advice that you'll find on Google.

Just like Superman never had a specific number of people that he had to save every day, you don't have a specific number of posts that you must create every day.

Step 2 | Plan a seven-day social media strategy that is truly individualized to best meet your needs.

YOU SHOWED UP.
NOW IT'S TIME TO SHOW OUT!

Today you will let me know that you made CEO Success Move #27 by sharing with me the details of your social media plan.

Inside of the companion course, there will be a link to an Instagram post related to this topic. Comment on this post to let me know which platform did you choose and how often you are planning to post. This is also a great way for you to see the social media plans of other edupreneurs as well.

DAY 28

ESSENTIALS OF A BUSINESS SOCIAL MEDIA PAGE

S uperman has the Fortress of Solitude. Batman has the Batcave. Iron Man has the basement in his mansion. You are a superhero, so where is your lair?

Many superheroes have a home base, and for your online business to be successful, you will need one too.

While superheroes use their home base to hide from the public, you will use yours to do the exact opposite. Your home base is where you will keep your Favorite Educators up to date with everything that's happening in your business.

As a new edupreneur, I made the mistake of believing that my home base had to be my own website. I spent weeks researching how to start a website and months trying to figure out how to actually create it using WordPress. I wasted A LOT of time that could have been much better spent building an engaged community, while also creating and promoting products. You know, those tasks that actually result in earning money rather than spending it.

If you're brand new to edupreneurship or you've been at it for a while but haven't started earning #CommaMoney (*i.e., $1,000+ every month*) yet, I strongly recommend that you skip the whole start a website thing for now and instead focus on building up a social media page for your business.

Yesterday you chose the social media platform that you'd engage on, and you created a weekly strategy. Today you're going to create a brand new account on that platform for your business.

Why do you need a separate account for your business? I'm glad you asked.

Unless you're living under a rock, you have at least one social media account. Even if you never post on it, you have one simply so that you can see what's happening in everyone else's life. I don't care if you've never posted or if you post every day; I do not recommend that you turn your personal social media account into your lair.

Even some of his closest friends didn't know that Clark Kent was Superman and if they had known, most of them wouldn't have believed or supported him anyway. As sad as it is, the truth of the matter is that most of your friends and family won't support your business, but that's ok because you're not creating it to help them. Don't let yourself fall into the trap or have your feelings hurt because your siblings, cousins, and best friends aren't supporting your business. Do your family and friends fall into the category of your Favorite Educator? If not, then your business is not for them, so don't get upset when they don't support it.

I highly recommend that you keep your personal account separate from your business account. In no way am I saying that you should not share personal details about yourself on your business account; however, I don't recommend that you share everything.

At the same time, I also don't recommend that you always show up on your business account perfectly polished. People want to see the real you. They want to see the real you that's awake and working on your business at 6 AM with no makeup on. They want to see the real you that has your hair in a ponytail because you're running outside playing with the kids.

Put on your cape, but keep it real at the same time. Think of your business social media page as the Daily Planet. Just like the Daily Planet highlighted stories of Superman saving the world while being unaware that in real life he was Clark Kent, your social media page will be the place where you capture highlights of how you're saving educators all around the world from their problems without them knowing everything about your real life.

CEO Success Move #28:

Create a social media page for your business

Your CEO Success Move for today is to create a social media page for your business. Be sure to capture your Expert Title and CEO Empowerment Statement on that page, and don't forget to add the link to your landing page and use it to invite people to join your community.

In Day 28 of the companion course, I take you behind the scenes of my Instagram page and explain how I'm able to include all of this information, even with a limited character count.

YOU SHOWED UP.

NOW IT'S TIME TO SHOW OUT!

Congratulations on starting your business social media page! Today you will Show Out by creating a post from your business social media page and tag me @ericaterryceo on Instagram + use the hashtag #ClassroomtoCEOin30days so that I can be one of your first followers and show your post some love!

DAY 29

PLAN YOUR 10-MINUTE EXPERT ENGAGEMENT PLAN

We're almost at the end of this 30-day journey together, and like any good teacher, I must assess whether or not you've met the standards.

To do so, guess what we're having today?

Yep, a Pop Quiz!

Grab a piece of paper and a pen/pencil and get ready to answer this question.

Are you ready?

Great! Here's your question:

_____ = Revenue

You can't remember? That's ok. It's an open book quiz, so feel free to use your notes or any other resources that are close by.

Shhhh…. I'll let you in on a little secret, but you can't share it with anyone else. You will probably find the correct answer in your Day 21 notes.

You got it right! Yay!!!!

Relationships = Revenue

Successful edupreneurs understand that they must dedicate time each week to nurture strong relationships within their community. You're here because you want to achieve success in building your online business, right?

Absolutely! This is why you're going to promise me that you will dedicate at least 10 minutes a day to nurturing relationships and engaging as an expert.

Promise?

Wait a minute…I hear you saying, '*Erica, I would love to spend 10 minutes a day nurturing relationships and engaging as an expert in my community, but I don't even have a community yet. I just started my business social media page yesterday, and right now, you and my mom are my only followers.*'

I hear you. It most definitely doesn't take 10 minutes a day to talk to your mom and me, which is why during today's CEO Success Move, you are going to craft a 10-minute Expert Engagement Plan that you will begin implementing tomorrow to successfully grow your audience.

CEO Success Move #29:

Engage as an Expert

Create a daily 10-minute Expert Engagement Plan.

The way in which you engage and the details of your Expert Engagement Plan will differ based on the social media platform that you chose on Day 27. Since the algorithms are constantly changing, I've included a video that provides expert engagement tips in the companion course that I will continue to update.

> # YOU SHOWED UP.
> # NOW IT'S TIME TO SHOW OUT!

Today you will let me know that you made Success Move #29 by engaging with me as an expert on Instagram.

Inside of the companion course, there will be a link to an Instagram post related to this topic. Comment on this post to let me know the platform that you will engage on daily and one of the action steps that you will take each day. This is also a great way for you to see the expert engagement plans of other edupreneurs as well.

DAY 30

BE SCARED, BUT DO IT ANYWAY

When you first opened this book, did you truly think it was possible for you to start a side hustle and launch your online business within 30 days?

Whether or not you believed it could really happen, you kept showing up, continued to make CEO Success Moves, and now, you are about to officially launch your new online business. Congratulations! I am soooo very proud of you!

While your online business may not be perfect or include all of the bells and whistles that you dream of, that's ok because perfection is never the goal. Done is better than perfect. Highlight that last sentence and hold it close to your heart because there will be plenty of days that you'll need to lean on it in order to keep moving forward. Your Classroom to CEO journey is all about empowering others to achieve success, and what you've created over the last thirty days will definitely achieve that goal!

OMG! Are you half as excited as I am? I'm over here doing a praise dance for you because I know that you are about to walk into your divine purpose and begin to empower other educators all over the world.

While I'm over here shouting, I can see that you're excited, but at the same time, you're as scared as a turkey in November.

I get it because I'm scared too. I feel like we've gotten to know each other well enough over the last thirty days that I can take off the mask and be fully transparent with you right now.

As I'm sitting here writing this chapter to encourage you to launch your new business, the truth is that I'm scared as hell. I've put off writing this final chapter for weeks because I know that once I finish it, there's no turning back, and the truth is that I'm afraid.

Thoughts that no one will buy this book or, even worse, those who buy it read the first few pages and think to themselves, '*this sucks*' continuously pop into my mind.

Thoughts that I don't have enough knowledge and expertise to write a side hustle startup book for educators fill my mind.

Thoughts that I'm going to fail keep creeping up on me.

I can't tell you the number of times I've had to read my scriptures and strike back so that I can encourage myself to keep moving forward. I know that if I can empower one educator to walk in purpose and create a life that they love, then it's worth it.

Earlier, when I made the reference that you're probably as scared as a turkey in November, I know that you're shaking in your boots right now because I am too. But here's what I also know to be true...

Unlike a scared turkey, when you launch your side hustle today, no one is going to come and eat you up. Just like they won't eat me up when I publish this book.

So let's make a pinky promise that today is the day that we will both be scared, but do it anyway.

Today is the day that you will launch your online business no matter what thoughts are roaming through your mind. You've been talking about your side hustle on social media for weeks. I've seen all of the social media posts that you've made teasing your followers about the upcoming launch of your new business.

Well, my friend, today is the big day, and now is the time to stop talking and start walking.

It's time to walk into your purpose.

It's time to walk into your destiny.

It's time to walk into being the top edupreneur in your subject area.

It's time to walk into EVERYTHING that you're meant to do and be as you move from the Classroom to CEO.

This is your moment, and I can't wait to see all of the wonderful things that are in store for you.

CEO Success Move #30:

Launch Your Online Business TODAY!

Today is the day to launch your new online business. I can't wait to celebrate with you! Check out Day 30 of the companion course to discover how you can join my next Classroom to CEO Launch Party!

YOU SHOWED UP.

NOW IT'S TIME TO SHOW OUT!

Allow me to be the first to congratulate you on launching your new business. Congratulations!!!! I am sooo super excited for you!

Create a social media post that shares this exciting news with everyone that you know. Be sure to tag me @ericaterryceo on Instagram + use the hashtag #ClassroomtoCEOin30days so that I can show your post mad love!

ABOUT THE AUTHOR

Erica Terry is an 18 year educator turned edupreneur and host of the *Classroom to CEO Podcast*. Through Classroom to CEO, she equips educators with profitable action steps to start a side hustle and create multiple streams of income.

With her unique background as a high school teacher, counselor, administrator and state/regional consultant, she shares exactly how she was able to use skills from each role in her educational journey to start a profitable online business and ultimately, kick the Sunday night blues to the curb. Erica is on a mission to empower educators, just like you, to create a legacy and life that they love waking up to on Monday mornings. Start your online business in the next 30 days at www.ClassroomtoCEO.com/30days.

EduMatch Publishing

CPSIA information can be obtained
at www.ICGtesting.com
Printed in the USA
FSHW020110220521
81706FS